ROOTS OF LYRIC

ROOTS OF LYRIC

Primitive Poetry and
Modern Poetics

BY ANDREW WELSH

Princeton University Press
Princeton, New Jersey

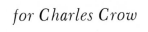

for Charles Crow

PREFACE

THIS STUDY started out to be a very simple thing. I was curious, as many others have been, to see whether there were some constants in the language of lyric poetry, some fundamental forms underlying the figures of imagery and the movements of sound and rhythm which so impressively characterize that language. There were. They did not, however, sit still for patient analysis. Those fundamental forms, the "roots" of lyric, were not at all as simple as they first appeared, and when approached too closely they began to shift, to turn into other things, and soon to divert attention from themselves by hinting at deeper roots—"ghostlier demarcations, keener sounds"—in poetic language. Thus this study transformed itself from a confident demonstration of recurring images and rhythms to a far more tentative speculation about the ways in which poetic language catches, reflects, and directs fundamental powers of vision and action.

The roots of lyric are not themselves lyric poems, but some understanding of the roots—the powers they derive from and the forms they take—lets us see the familiar elements of poetic language in new, and sometimes strange, ways. In this study the roots are first seen as they are embodied in the riddles, charms, and chants of primitive and folk poetry; then they are followed through stages of fuller development in Renaissance emblem books, Japanese haiku, and the satires of John Skelton; they are still recognizable, and still illuminating, in Chinese poems, Image poems by Pound and Williams, and in complex lyric poetry by Yeats, Wyatt, and Hopkins.

The author is not now and never has been a specialist in

modern poetry or Renaissance lyric, much less in Chinese linguistics or Navaho ritual. That there are specialists in those and other areas makes possible speculations such as mine, and I have used their work gratefully. The texts of primitive poetry which appear in chapters six and seven are not the results of my own fieldwork or of unusually obscure research, and they were not selected with the idea of making a particular critical point; many of them were first suggested to me by anthologized translations of primitive literatures or by books such as C. M. Bowra's *Primitive Song*, and once they were traced back to the transcriptions and commentaries of the original collectors the texts made their own critical points. The sources are handled in the notes, but I would like to acknowledge here a more general debt to three scholars, the folklorist Archer Taylor and the literary critics Northrop Frye and Hugh Kenner, who cast shadows longer than any footnotes can accommodate. This book has received generous support from The Research Council and the Faculty Academic Study Program of Rutgers University, and it was finished with the help of an Andrew Mellon Postdoctoral Fellowship at the University of Pittsburgh, where the Faculty of Arts and Sciences and the staff of the Hillman Library provided comfort and assistance. Special thanks go to Dan Howard for making studies such as this one possible, to Princeton University Press editor Marjorie Sherwood for several years of patience, encouragement, and help, and to John Seidman for help in thinking about the ideas in chapter four. My greatest debt is to an incomparable teacher, scholar, and friend; to him this book is humbly dedicated.

CONTENTS

LIST OF ABBREVIATIONS

CWC   Ernest Fenollosa, *The Chinese Written Character as a Medium for Poetry*, ed. Ezra Pound (San Francisco: City Lights, 1964)

ER   Archer Taylor, *English Riddles from Oral Tradition* (Berkeley and Los Angeles: Univ. of California Press, 1951)

IR   Vernam Hull and Archer Taylor, *A Collection of Irish Riddles*, Folklore Studies, 6 (Berkeley and Los Angeles: Univ. of California Press, 1955)

JAF   *Journal of American Folklore*

LR   Archer Taylor, *The Literary Riddle before 1600* (Berkeley and Los Angeles: Univ. of California Press, 1948)

PMLA   *Publications of the Modern Language Association of America*

ROOTS OF LYRIC

I. COORDINATES

WHAT IS the poet's language? asked Wordsworth in the Preface to the 1800 edition of the *Lyrical Ballads*. His answer has become an important bench mark in the history of literary criticism: a poet is "a man speaking to men" and his language is "a selection of the language really spoken by men." It is true, Wordsworth said, that the poet is more sensitive and more imaginative than most men, and that his poetic language arises from occasions of particular excitement and passion. Yet there is still no essential difference between the language of poetry and the language of good prose. Poetry uses meter, of course, but this is something added to temper the words should the natural passion of the poet be too strong, to boost the words with traditional associations should his language be too weak for the occasion, and, in general, something to mark the selecting process by which the poet adopts and purifies the raw language. It is nothing that should restrict the poet's choice of subject or cut him off from the natural language of men. Other poetic devices, such as metaphors and appropriate "figures," may also arise naturally in the language from the poet's passions, but he will not shock the reader with unnatural, artificial, or incongruous images. These latter are among the "abuses" introduced into the language of poetry by a degenerate age, Wordsworth added in his appendix to the Preface in 1802, for, as the language of poetry moved further and further away from the language of natural excitement that was used by the earliest poets, it "became daily more and more corrupt, thrusting out of sight the plain humanities of nature by a motley masquerade of tricks, quaintnesses, hieroglyphics, and enigmas."

3

Wordsworth's answers to his own question have had their troubles, not the least of them raised by his friend Coleridge in chapter seventeen of the *Biographia Literaria.* If we follow Wordsworth and look in "low and rustic life" for the natural language really spoken by men, Coleridge said uneasily, we are likely to find a language of unreflective literalness that lacks the creative connections made by language in its best poetic use. Any thoughtful answer to Wordsworth's question will in fact present a series of new questions. If the language of poetry is a selection of natural speech, then what do we mean by "selection," or by "natural," or, for that matter, by "speech"? The initial question, however, remains, if not to be finally settled then at least to be asked and answered again and again. What is the language of poetry? And the corollary question: are the familiar devices of rhythm, metaphor, and poetic diction an essential part of this language, or are they merely ornamental and perhaps morally suspect? Wordsworth might well have asked himself the question again on 24 May 1812, when, during a walk with Crabb Robinson in the fields north of Oxford Road, Robinson read him a number of poems by William Blake. One of the poems was almost certainly the one Blake lyric that had already gained a small reputation, a poem in which, as any child can tell, the natural language of poetry is clearly heard:

The Tyger

Tyger Tyger, burning bright,
In the forests of the night;
What immortal hand or eye,
Could frame thy fearful symmetry?

In what distant deeps or skies,
Burnt the fire of thine eyes?
On what wings dare he aspire?
What the hand, dare seize the fire?

And what shoulder, & what art,
Could twist the sinews of thy heart?
And when thy heart began to beat,
What dread hand? & what dread feet?

What the hammer? what the chain,
In what furnace was thy brain?
What the anvil? what dread grasp,
Dare its deadly terrors clasp?

When the stars threw down their spears
And water'd heaven with their tears:
Did he smile his work to see?
Did he who made the Lamb make thee?

Tyger Tyger burning bright,
In the forests of the night:
What immortal hand or eye,
Dare frame thy fearful symmetry?

Robinson noted in his diary that Wordsworth was pleased
with some of the Blake poems and that "he regarded Blake
as having in him the elements of poetry much more than
either Byron or Scott."[1] The two literary men then met
with a literary woman, Miss Joanna Baillie, and accom-
panied her home ("a model of an English gentlewoman,"
Wordsworth commented). Robinson closes his diary entry
without any further discussion of the poems, and closes the
book on what appears to be the fullest recorded piece of
Wordsworthian criticism on Blake.

If Wordsworth ever again paid close attention to Blake's
poetry, and to "The Tyger" in particular, his thoughts are
probably lost to us beyond recovery. Poets and critics since
then, however, have not been so reticent, and critical discussion of "The Tyger" abounds. The poem, a simple lyric
with troubling complexities, does invite discussion, and it
offers many paths to follow. An approach to the poem can
begin simply, perhaps with a descriptive commentary of

"what the poem is about": it is easy enough to see that it opens with the creation of a fierce animal, and that by the end it has led us up to the philosophical question of whether the dreaded tiger and the gentle lamb can be creations of the same creator. But then other meanings in the poem come into view, such as those implied by the choice of imagery. It is interesting to notice, for example, that the creator is given in strongly corporeal images—laboring shoulder, planted feet, hammer-wielding hand. These images build a tonality of power, a purposeful power strong enough to forge—and then perhaps to reconcile—the Tyger and the Lamb. Then another familiar path: who is the speaker in the poem? Is it a child whose voice betrays a growing terror in confronting the burning Tyger, is it a man like us, unable to comprehend the existence of such contraries as Tyger and Lamb, or is it a visionary prophet who can see beyond our limited state to a reconciliation of these apparent opposites? Soon the historical and political contexts may begin to resonate through the poem: it was probably written in the fall of 1792, when across the English Channel the fiery creation of the French Revolution was devouring the counterrevolutionary forces of church and state. A genetic approach to the poem is possible as well, if we look at Blake's earlier drafts. There is a rejected stanza to wonder about; the present fifth stanza, we would also notice, was added later in a brilliant afterthought; there is a small but striking change in that the creator's "smile" was first a "laugh."

After finding a way through all this, the reader can discover still wider perspectives of meaning opening up. The poem takes its place in the *Songs of Innocence and of Experience* and in Blake's work as a whole so that the wondering speaker takes on the characteristics of a fallen Urizen, the blacksmith-creator is seen as the Eternal Prophet, Los, whose hammer can create the glowing sun, and the capitulating stars are seen as signaling the defeat of the mechanical, Newtonian "single vision" of the universe. The poem is

related to the rest of literature as well: the creator has over-
tones of Daedalus, Prometheus, and Vulcan; the spear-carry-
ing stars may recall a war in heaven and the angelic legions
of Lucifer; the "forests of the night" are related to all the
dark woods, blasted heaths, trackless oceans, and other waste
lands in literature which, like Dante's *selva oscura*, can also
be forests of the mind. The Tyger itself carries some of the
meanings of the Biblical (and Melvillean) Leviathan or
Beowulf's night-gliding monsters, or it may become a fiery
beast of apocalypse, a "tyger of wrath," in the manner of the
Old Testament prophets. Finally, the poem can be seen in
the context of *all* creative processes as a microcosm of the
universal act of creation which unites opposing principles
(Light and Dark, Good and Evil, Yin and Yang) into vital
existence. Viewed in this way, the poem presents an almost
scriptural vision of the act of creation—Blake's own creation
included.[2]

All these prospects and many more are found in the poem
—yet a problem arises for anyone who is still thinking of
Wordsworth's question. None of the commentaries has ques-
tioned the language of the poem: none of them, in fact, has
given even any indication that this is a lyric poem and not
a novel, a drama, an epic, or an interesting and possibly
heretical fragment of scripture. Although Wordsworth was
not asking about lyric poetry only, I would like to specialize
his question and ask what it is that makes "The Tyger" dis-
tinctively a lyric poem, with a distinctive language.

Looking back at the poem, then, and leaving large questions of meaning aside for a while, we find several basic elements that are not usually found in other forms of literary
art. The rhythm of the language is one of these. Wordsworth
conceded that the language of poetry differs somewhat from
the spoken language by its use of meter, and in this poem
the language is arranged to follow what can be formally
described as the falling rhythm of trochaic meter (though
the trochaic lines are curtailed, and some lines are unmis-
takably iambic). Yet we can also hear, as Blake meant us

to hear, a basic four-beat rhythm that recalls the nursery rhymes and game-songs of children:

> ´   ´   ´   ´
> Tyger Tyger, burning bright,
> ´   ´   ´   ´
> In the forests of the night . . .
>
> ´   ´   ´   ´
> Bobby Shafto's gone to sea,
> ´   ´   ´   ´
> Silver buckles at his knee . . .
>
> ´   ´   ´   ´
> Cobbler, cobbler, mend my shoe,
> ´   ´   ´   ´
> Yea, good master, that I'll do . . .[3]

It is the rhythm of song-verse, in which the one-two-three-four of the steady beat is far more important in determining the movement of the language than the consistently repeated patterns and counted syllables of foot-prosody. And along with this steady beat of the song-rhythm are other rhythmical movements set up by repeated sounds in the language itself, the repeated words, the alliterations, assonances, rhymes, and other sound-echoes woven through the texture of "The Tyger":

Tyger	. . .	*Tyger*
*b*urning	. . .	*b*right
*T*yger	. . .	b*r*ight
*f*rame	. . .	*f*ear*f*ul
twi*s*t	. . .	*s*in*e*ws
ch*ain*	. . .	br*ain*

Together, the song-rhythm and the internal rhythms growing out of the sounds in words create something that is quite different from the rhythm of a man speaking to men. What can be heard in the poem, perhaps, is the rhythm of man speaking to other-than-man, as it is heard in a children's charm:

> Rain, rain, go away,
> Come again another day . . .

in a children's prayer:

8

> Now I lay me down to sleep
> I pray the Lord my soul to keep . . .

and in a liturgical hymn:

> *Dies irae, dies illa* . . .

Questions of meaning are finally not left aside at all, but are engaged on a level unique to lyric poetry, for the language of Blake's poem seems to have built into it rhythms that can simultaneously call up the rhythms of innocent nursery rhymes and game-songs and the rhythms of magic incantation, epiphanic invocation, and prophetic hymn.

These elements of the lyric language speak to what may be called the aural imagination, a listener's perception of sounds moving successively in time. There are other elements, however, which are aligned more with the visual imagination, elements which work toward imagery in the sense of picture and spatial form. The little coiled spring *y*, for example, which Blake placed inside his Tyger, is a visual element that belongs to the emblematic tradition of poetry, & in choosing the ampersand, which represents a meaning rather than a sound, Blake used one of the few English ideographs. Both devices were familiar enough usages in Blake's time, but nevertheless he did have a choice, and he chose to use them. He engraved the poem several times on copper plates along with his engraved pictures of a tiger and a bare tree, involving the poetic text with a visual design in a "composite art" that again has roots in the emblem tradition. The visual imagination in poetry, moreover, is not limited to an engraved poem, and "The Tyger" shows it working on other levels as well. Metaphor is one of these, the process which places the brain of the Tyger on the anvil and which causes the stars to weep. Beyond this, there is a process which creates a hierarchy of imagery, a spatial structuring which first juxtaposes the toughness of the blacksmith and his forge with the heart and brain of the Tyger, which next juxtaposes this com-

9

plex with the images of the frightened stars and the meek
Lamb of Innocence, and which places all of this under the
mysterious smile of the creator.

The hierarchy of imagery is as much conceptualization
as it is picture or spatial form, and we find that the pictorial pattern and the intellectual pattern are very closely
connected. The poem is made up of a series of questions,
questions which, working against the forward motion of
the rhythms, hold up the poem while the imagination tries
to visualize—or conceptualize—the answers. The questions
are deceptively simple at first, like those of the enigma tradition in popular literature ("And what shoulder, & what
art . . . ?"), but by the end of the poem the questioning
has developed into the complete religious paradox familiar
to the poetry of meditation ("Did he who made the Lamb
make thee?"). Somehow the processes of thinking and the
structures of completed thought—question and answer—
are, along with image and spatial form, basic elements of
the visual imagination in this poem. And somehow Wordsworth's "abuses" of poetic language, "hieroglyphics and
enigmas," lie waiting at the roots of a poem he heard read
on a pleasant May day in 1812.

It can be argued that these small elements of the aural
and visual imaginations are basic particles in the language
of poetry and that their relationships constitute its basic
structure. According to this view they are not artificial and
degenerate abuses of the natural language of poetry, or
mere ornaments hung on that language, but actual sources
of the language. It is a view that tends to be more popular
with poets than with critics, it seems, and whatever Wordsworth the critic had to say about the artifices of poetic language, Wordsworth the poet was certainly aware of the fundamental importance of these structures of sound and image.
In *The Prelude* (1805), for example, we can watch his own
visual imagination drawing a picture of Revolutionary
Paris with images of tigers and forests of the night:

10

a place of fear
Unfit for the repose which night requires,
Defenceless as a wood where Tygers roam.

But perhaps a clearer example of a poet who believed that
the language of poetry has its source in the relationships of
these small elements is William Carlos Williams:

> It is in the minutiae—in the minute organization of
> the words and their relationships in a composition that
> the seriousness and value of a work of writing exist—
> *not* in the sentiments, ideas, schemes portrayed.
> It is here, furthermore, that creation takes place. It
> is not a plaster of thought applied.[4]

The creative roots of "The Tyger," Williams would say,
are seen far more in the levels of rhythm and image organizing the words and their relationships than in the philosophical, literary, or historical meanings—rich as they are—
which also reverberate through the finished poem.

Two interesting accounts by poets of the places where
creation takes place describe more specifically the kinds of
powers at work when words are organized into the language of poetry. Both poets tell of experiencing impulses
which they recognized as the beginnings of poetic composition. Both experiences took place at extreme boundaries
of poetic language, and for this reason they were particularly revealing about the powers and conditions involved.
Paul Valéry describes the struggles of the aural imagination
to engender poetry, struggles that were most revealing
when on one occasion they were completely unsuccessful.
Ezra Pound tells how the very different powers of the visual
imagination once presented him with the beginnings of a
poem, and with poetic difficulties far beyond anything he
had expected.

Valéry begins his account by noting that certain poems
he had written "had as a starting point merely one of these
impulses of the 'formative' sensibility which are anterior to

any 'subject' or to any finite, expressible idea." One poem, for example, "began merely with the hint of a rhythm, *which gradually acquired a meaning.*" Once, however, a combination of rhythms came to him that did not, and could not, lead to a poem:

> I had left my house to find, in walking and looking about me, relaxation from some tedious work. As I went along my street, which mounts steeply, I was *gripped* by a rhythm which took possession of me and soon gave me the impression of some force outside myself. Another rhythm overtook and combined with the first, and certain strange *transverse relations* were set up between them. This combination, which went far beyond anything I could have expected from my rhythmic faculties, made the sense of strangeness, which I have mentioned, almost unbearable. I argued that there had been an error of person, that this grace had descended on the wrong head, since I could make no use of a gift which, in a musician, would doubtless have assumed a lasting shape, and it was in vain that these two themes offered me a composition whose sequence and complexity amazed my ignorance and reduced it to despair. The magic suddenly vanished after about twenty minutes, leaving me on the bank of the Seine, as perplexed as the duck in the fable, which saw a swan emerge from the egg she had hatched.

In some cases, wordless rhythms can become an organizing power for words. Valéry, no stranger to language organized by rhythm, goes on to realize that he was in fact accustomed to having the rhythms of walking bring him "a quickened flow of ideas," which means to him material that he knows how to handle, material for a poem. But a poet requires language for his art, and this time "my movements assailed my consciousness through a subtle arrangement of rhythms, instead of provoking that amalgam of

12

images, inner words, and virtual acts that one calls an Idea." The combination of mental rhythms he heard, however, was itself a development of the same basic organizing power, the same impulse of the "formative sensibility": "What was I to think? I fancied that the mental activity produced by walking was probably related to a general stimulus that found its outlet as best it could in the brain; and that this kind of quantitative function could be as well fulfilled by the emission of some rhythm as by verbal images or some sort of symbols; and, further, that, at a certain point in my mental processes, all ideas, rhythms, images, and memories or inventions were merely *equivalents*."[5] The organizing power is based in, or in some deep way related to, a physical action, the physical rhythm of walking. It is not a simple relationship, but it was clear to Valéry that the same power may develop at one time into "a subtle arrangement of rhythms" in his mind, and at other times into the organized words, images, ideas, and memories of poetry. Although on this occasion nothing came over into the area of language, the experience nevertheless permitted him to see the organizing powers of his aural imagination at work, and to see at the source of those powers the rhythm of a physical action.

Compare this with Ezra Pound's experience in the same city, where the initiative of a poem came to him not as pure rhythm but as pure image or pattern:

Three years ago in Paris I got out of a "metro" train at La Concorde, and saw suddenly a beautiful face, and then another and another, and then a beautiful child's face, and then another beautiful woman, and I tried all that day to find words for what this had meant to me, and I could not find any words that seemed to me worthy, or as lovely as that sudden emotion. And that evening, as I went home along the Rue Raynouard, I was still trying and I found, suddenly, the expression. I do not mean that I found words, but there came an equation . . . not in speech, but in little splotches of colour. It was just that—a "pattern," or hardly a pattern, if by "pattern" you mean something with a "repeat" in it. But it was a word, the beginning, for me, of a language in colour.

At the basis of Pound's impulse was a moment of complex perception, rather than the rhythm of a physical action. Although he eventually managed to make a poem of it— the famous Imagist poem "In a Station of the Metro"— Pound also wrote that "my experience in Paris should have gone into paint. If instead of colour I had perceived sound or planes in relation, I should have expressed it in music or in sculpture. Colour was, in that instance, the 'primary pigment'; I mean that it was the first adequate equation that came into consciousness."[6]

Both Pound and Valéry experienced the beginnings of some kind of fundamental organization. For Pound it came in the images and patterns of the visual imagination, and for Valéry it came in the counterpointed rhythms of the aural imagination. Perhaps, as Pound suggested, such impulses first emerge into consciousness in some primary form, some "primary pigment" of seeing or hearing, and perhaps, as Valéry felt, there is an even earlier point at which such impulses treat those different pigments as being merely equivalents. Yet when they do emerge in the consciousness of a poet, rather than of a painter or a musician, his job of course is to direct them into language, "to find words," if it is possible, that will express the original impulse and be worthy of it.

The exploration of the subconscious depths in poets is probably best left to another discipline, and literary criticism is primarily concerned with how the impulses arising from those depths have been caught and transformed in language. When Williams wrote that creation takes place "in the minute organization of the words and their relationships" he was writing about Pound's early Cantos, and

14

Pound is the poet who can give us some coordinates for speaking about the organization of poetic language. He first of all pointed out how such language often borders on the realms of music or the visual arts, reflecting basic powers of the aural or visual imaginations. "There have always been two sorts of poetry," he wrote, "which are, for me at least, the most 'poetic'; they are firstly, the sort of poetry which seems to be music just forcing itself into articulate speech, and secondly, that sort of poetry which seems as if sculpture or painting were just forced or forcing itself into words."[7]

The "two sorts of poetry" represent two fundamental ways of organizing the language of poetry, and both ways appear in the language of a poem such as "The Tyger." They define what are actually an axis of the aural imagination and an axis of the visual imagination in poetic language. But there appears to be a third dimension to this language as well, for Pound elsewhere distinguished three ways of what he called "charging language with meaning":

> If we chuck out the classifications which apply to the outer shape of the work, or to its occasion, and if we look at what actually happens, in, let us say, poetry, we will find that the language is charged or energized in various manners.
>
> That is to say, there are three "kinds of poetry":
>
> MELOPOEIA, wherein the words are charged, over and above their plain meaning, with some musical property, which directs the bearing or trend of that meaning.
>
> PHANOPOEIA, which is a casting of images upon the visual imagination.
>
> LOGOPOEIA, "the dance of the intellect among words," that is to say, it employs words not only for their direct meaning, but it takes count in a special way of habits of usage, of the context we *expect* to find with the word, its usual concomitants, of its known acceptances, and of ironical play. It holds the aesthetic content

15

which is peculiarly the domain of verbal manifestation, and cannot possibly be contained in plastic or in
music.

There are, then, three organizing powers in the language of
poetry: "melopoeia," the making of music, "phanopoeia,"
the making of the bright image, and "logopoeia," the making of the resonant word. Some poetry will reflect one power
more than others, and when he looked back on the history
of lyric poetry Pound saw the power of melopoeia greatest
in Greek and Provençal lyrics, the highest attainment of
phanopoeia in Chinese poetry, and the sophisticated use of
logopoeia in the Latin of Propertius and the French of
Laforgue. He felt, moreover, that these powers charge not
only the language of lyric poetry but the language of all
literary art, whether lyric or epic, drama or prose: "All writing is built up of these three elements, plus 'architectonics'
or 'the form of the whole.' "[8] And for Pound, as for Williams, it is the line-by-line workings of these elements, the
kinds of organization that were brought out on our return
to the Blake poem, for example, that tell us most about the
poet's distinctive language.

Pound's three kinds of poetic language were scarcely a new
discovery. The familiar categories of sound, image, and word
cover some of the same territory, though usually without
Pound's sense of powers that charge the language of poetry
with unique kinds of meaning. The immediate source of his
distinctions seems to be Coleridge, who, in the essay "On the
Principles of Genial Criticism," spoke of "poetry of the
ear," "poetry of the eye," and "poetry of language."[9] In
Coleridge, however, these do not refer to forms of poetic
language but to much broader distinctions among the arts
themselves. As things "made" by the creative imagination,
all the fine arts were for Coleridge different species of "poetry," and in his essay "poetry of the ear" means simply
music, "poetry of the eye" means painting and sculpture.
There was a set of distinctions known well by the neoclas-

sical poets and critics of the eighteenth century, however, which did refer to the language of poetry, and which they were likely to call "verse" (that is, "versification"), "imagination" (in the pre-Romantic meaning of an associative faculty which discovers resemblances between things and which produces mental or verbal pictures), and "diction"— or, as Pope named them in the *Essay on Criticism* (vv. 289-383), "numbers," "wit" (again meaning the faculty which sees resemblances and produces poetic "conceits"), and "language" ("expression," "style"). If there is some ultimate source for these kinds of trinities it may well be Aristotle's *Poetics*, which distinguishes three of the six elements of the art of tragedy as *melos* (μέλος), *opsis* (ὄψις), and *lexis* (λέξις). In tragic drama, the only form of poetry that Aristotle treats specifically, they refer simply to "music" (or "song"), "spectacle" (costumes, scenery), and "diction" (*Poetics* 6.1450a7-15, 1450b13-20).

In one form or another, then, the distinctions have been familiar and useful to criticism for some time. But to Pope these elements of poetic language were mere techniques which only limited or capricious critics would emphasize, and to Aristotle they were three elements of tragedy of far less concern or importance than the major elements of plot, character, and thought. More recently, F. R. Leavis has said that Pound's distinctions of melopoeia, phanopoeia, and logopoeia are naive and can tell us little about poetry.[10] Yet modern poetry and criticism, which have become particularly interested in the language of poetry, seem nevertheless to require some version of these coordinates to describe the peculiar dimensions of that language, and Pound's formulations are a good place to begin.

One work of modern criticism which makes use of these distinctions is Northrop Frye's *Anatomy of Criticism*, and here we find some additional suggestions for our own study. Although Frye uses Aristotle's terminology rather than Pound's, his sense of those terms clearly extends them toward Pound's three ways of charging language with meaning. *Melos, opsis,* and *lexis* (corresponding to Pound's melopoeia, phanopoeia, and logopoeia) belong to what Frye calls the "literal" phase of meaning in a work of literature. Criticism attending to this phase of meaning considers the work as simply a structure of interrelated motifs, a group of organized words—rather than, say, as a document which reflects historical events or philosophical ideas (the "descriptive" phase of meaning), or as an overall form which presents a mimesis, a unified "imitation" of human action or thought (the "formal" phase of meaning). The descriptive and formal phases of meaning, as well as others, are of course present in the finished work and are also important concerns of literary criticism, but Frye agrees with Williams that the minute organization of the words and their relationships is the center and source of literary art, and with Pound that the powers of the aural and visual imaginations define two key principles of that minute organization. The "real core of poetry," he writes, is not descriptive meaning, and not the poet's *cri de coeur* (which is a description of an emotion), but "a subtle and elusive verbal pattern that avoids, and does not lead to, such bald statements" (p. 81). *Melos,* for Frye, is the musical principle of verbal organization, and it involves rhythm, the sounds of words, and the shaping, temporal movements associated with the ear. *Opsis,* the visual principle, involves imagery, pattern, and the containing, spatial, and conceptual configurations associated with the eye.

In lyric poetry, the creative sources of *melos* and *opsis* are two subconscious impulses that Frye whimsically names "babble" and "doodle." "Babble" begins with a rhythmical initiative which, when it connects with language, starts to shape the sound-associations of words into elements of rhyme, assonance, alliteration, and punning. Valéry seems to have discovered the impulses of "babble" at work, though in his case they remained purely musical. "Doodle," the subconscious source of *opsis,* begins in the playful association of images, structures, and meanings, and it emerges in language as verbal design, the patterns of the visual imagination in poetry (pp. 274-78). Pound saw a pattern of faces in a metro station, and he doodled all day with patterns in language that might express it. Frye goes on to suggest that we can recognize in the language of lyric poetry two fundamental forms which are the basic expressions of the processes of "babble" and "doodle" respectively, and which are the root forms, or "radicals," of lyrical *melos* and *opsis*. The radical of *melos* is *charm*:

> the hypnotic incantation that, through its pulsing dance rhythm, appeals to involuntary physical response, and is hence not far from the sense of magic, or physically compelling power. The etymological descent of charm from *carmen*, song, may be noted. Actual charms have a quality that is imitated in popular literature by work songs of various kinds, especially lullabies, where the drowsy sleep-inducing repetition shows the underlying oracular or dream pattern very clearly. Invective or flyting, the literary imitation of the spell-binding curse, uses similar incantatory devices for opposite reasons. . . .   (pp. 278-79)

The radical of *opsis* is *riddle*: "a fusion of sensation and reflection, the use of an object of sense experience to stimulate a mental activity in connection with it. Riddle was originally the cognate object of read, and the riddle seems intimately involved with the whole process of reducing language to visible form, a process which runs through such by-forms of riddle as hieroglyphic and ideogram" (p. 280). Finally, Frye notes that these fundamental forms of poetic language have old associations with magic which correspond to the *melos* powers of motion and the *opsis* powers of spatial containment: "Just as the charm is not far from a sense of magical compulsion, so the curiously wrought object, whether sword-hilt or illuminated manuscript, is not far from a sense of enchantment or magical imprisonment" (p. 280).

And where is *lexis*, or Pound's logopoeia? In both Pound and Frye this element occupies an anomalous position with respect to the other two. Pound does not mention it when he speaks of the two sorts of poetry which are the most fundamentally "poetic," those which seem to be either music or visual art just forcing itself into articulate speech. Yet it appears as one of his three ways of charging language with meaning—and it holds, moreover, "the aesthetic content which is peculiarly the domain of verbal manifestation." Frye points out, simply and neatly, that *lexis* covers *all* the language of poetry; it is what *melos* and *opsis* both ultimately become in a verbal art. "Considered as a verbal structure," he writes, "literature presents a *lexis* which combines two other elements: *melos*, an element analogous to or otherwise connected with music, and *opsis*, which has a similar connection with the plastic arts. The word *lexis* itself may be translated 'diction' when we are thinking of it as a narrative sequence of sounds caught by the ear, and as 'imagery' when we are thinking of it as forming a simultaneous pattern of meaning apprehended in an act of mental 'vision' " (p. 244). In talking about the roots of melopoeia and phanopoeia in the language of poetry, then, as we are about to do, we are also exploring the roots of logopoeia, or *lexis*. Like the space and time of physics, the space and time of poetics are finally two faces of the same thing.

Williams, Pound, and Frye all seem to lead us to lyric for poetic language with the deepest roots. It is lyric, Frye writes, that "most clearly shows the hypothetical core of literature, narrative and meaning in their literal aspects as word-order and word-pattern" (p. 271). Although other forms of literature tap the same sources, the language of those forms is finally organized according to other principles. The language of a novel, for example, depends most of all on the semantic organization of prose, sentences which "make sense." Most long narrative poems have required a consistent meter which organizes the language into regular verse-lines, and in oral epics further organizes it into fixed patterns of formulaic diction. Lyric, however, if it chooses, can keep free of such demands, staying close to language charged with the fundamental powers of melopoeia and phanopoeia for its final as well as initial basis of growth and organization. Lyric is finally less a particular genre of poetry than a distinctive way of organizing language, and we can see in Williams' *Paterson* and Pound's *Cantos* that there are basic conflicts between the traditional demands of a long poem and the very different organization of a lyric-centered language.

Pound's melopoeia, phanopoeia, and logopoeia name three powers of lyric-centered language, and we will keep his names, though not his descriptions, of those powers. They locate ways of organizing language that can be investigated further, but a virtue of his definitions is that they are undeveloped enough to leave us room to maneuver, and room to expand the definitions as the maneuverings progress. The definition of phanopoeia as "a casting of images upon the visual imagination" obviously leaves unstated much else that this power does in organizing the language of a poem such as "The Tyger," and the definition of melopoeia as something wherein the words are charged "with some musical property" calls for a closer look at just what musical properties are available in the resources of language, and what forms they take in the language of poetry. One element of Pound's formulations that will not be left behind, however, is his key sense that these are not merely ornamental techniques but fundamental powers that form the language and direct the meanings of poetry.

Northrop Frye's suggestions are also adapted to our own purposes. Frye conceives of *melos* and *opsis* as the musical and visual extremes of a single axis of *lexis*, rather than as powers defining a complete set of coordinates for the language of poetry, but we can change his geometry without seriously distorting his meanings. His definitions of *charm* and *riddle* as the radicals of lyric *melos* and *opsis* will not serve for the actual charms and riddles of primitive and folk literature, nor were they intended to. They are a literary theorist's conception of what the root forms of the language of lyric poetry must, in some hypothetical way, look like. Yet they suggest where to begin looking for those forms, in the collections and studies made by ethnologists and folklorists of actual charms and riddles. In this book, however, the investigations into those and other radicals of the language of lyric poetry involve us in speculations that are finally well outside of Frye's "literal" phase of meaning, and outside any view of poetry as an inward organization of words only. A vocabulary for these speculations must come from Aristotle, for the radicals of lyric melopoeia and phanopoeia seem themselves to have roots deeply connected with powers of action and seeing in human experience, and with praxis and mimesis in language.

In this study, then, Wordsworth's central question— What is the poet's language?—is asked again, and some answers are sought by exploring increasingly complex developments of the powers of lyric melopoeia and phanopoeia. The power of phanopoeia is explored first, beginning with the folk riddle and two closely related literary forms, the literary riddle and the kenning. The roots of phanopoeia are seen raised to higher powers in the Renaissance emblem, in Japanese and Chinese poetry, and in modern poems by Pound, Williams, and Yeats. Finally, Fenollosa's theory of the ideogram presents a poetics based on the powers of phanopoeia. The second part of the study proposes that there are three roots of lyric melopoeia. One of them is in fact heard in the rhythms and sounds of primitive charms, but another is heard in the rhythms of dance-songs, whether primitive or courtly, and a third in the rhythms of Wordsworth's poet as a man speaking to men. Each of the three roots of melopoeia is derived—or so I will argue —from a different use of language and is characterized by a different rhythmical organization. The melopoeia of poetry again raises these roots to higher powers, but principally it combines them into more complex forms of organization. The communal chants of primitive poetry show the early stages of this process, and they also present particularly interesting demonstrations of some of the powers of rhythmical language. More complex combinations are heard in the poetry of John Skelton, and the poems of Sir Thomas Wyatt bring us to the fully developed music of English lyric poetry. There we come to an ending, except for a short coda. The further development of the powers of phanopoeia and melopoeia into logopoeia, or the *lexis* of poetry, soon reaches beyond the recognizable roots of lyric, and beyond the limits of this book.

One more point to be made by way of introduction concerns the use of "primitive" forms of poetry. The phrase "primitive poetry" is used here only as a convenient and general term; many of the texts do in fact come from what are usually called "primitive" (or "preliterate," or "preindustrial," or "nontechnological") societies, but others are from "folk" cultures, and still others from different stages of the "popular" literature of our own culture. There are dangers, of course, in using many of these texts at all, for they take us quickly beyond the more familiar paths of literary criticism into foreign and remote areas of language and culture. There we must find guides as best we can and depend on their specialized knowledges of those regions. Throughout, however, "primitive" does not mean "primal." We know that the languages of primitive societies are not in any way "younger" in time or "simpler" in form than other languages; similarly, it cannot be assumed that "primitive poetry" represents anything but complex and highly developed uses of those languages. It has often developed the roots of poetry differently than our own traditions have, however, and that is one reason it interests us. Our search is not for primal sources but for basic structures of poetic language, whether they are found in a Bantu riddle or a poem by Donne, in a Cherokee charm or a song by Shakespeare. If the poetics of one leads us in some suggestive way to the poetics of the other, we will have discovered something about the language of poetry without involving ourselves in either genetic or psychological assumptions.

It should be admitted, finally, that the primitive poetry in this book is not regarded simply as a means to a literary critic's obscure (or familiar) ends. Although we remain strangers to much that is in these texts, they are often striking poems in themselves which cannot fail to move and delight even outsiders. One thing, at least, quickly becomes clear at the outset. The language of primitive poetry is neither the "natural" speech of Wordsworth's impassioned poet nor the unreflective literalness that Coleridge anticipated; it is far more complex, and far more interesting, than either of these. First, then, let us begin with those elements of language so little appreciated by Wordsworth, the hieroglyphics and enigmas which lie near the roots of the power of phanopoeia in lyric poetry.

II. RIDDLE

ADAM'S FIRST JOB in the Garden, the story goes, was to find names for the creatures of his world. An unsurpassed Master of Riddles brought to him the beasts of the field and every fowl of the air to see how he would name them— ready, we can imagine, to confront him with the tiger soon after the lamb. It was part of Adam's education, a teaching based on the theory that to find the name of something it is necessary to know it, and to know something it is necessary to see it with clarity. With clear eyesight and a clear mind and a clear language there is no trouble: Adam at that time had all three, and the names he found for the birds and beasts were, the story continues, the right names. In that world there were none of the obstacles and side-tracks lying between perception and cognition that so trouble and enliven our own struggles with namings.

All our languages, post-Eden and post-Babel as they are, still seem to carry memories of that old dream, teasing us from time to time with hints of the lost clarity and unbroken connections of Adam's vision. The Greek verb οἶδα means "I know," but it is the verb for "see," cognate with Latin *vidēre*, and the form is not the simple present but a present perfect: an aspect of the verb that implies completed action, something that has been done thoroughly, whose effects can continue into the present. "I know" is "I have seen." The cognate in Old English is *(ic) wāt*, from the infinitive *witan* (the ancestor of Pope's word "wit"). It too means "I know," yet again it is not a present form but, in this case, a preterite, and behind the meaning "I know" again stands the older perfective meaning "I have seen." In a different way another English word, the archaic but once rich word "ken," could also hint at seeing and knowing as a single process. When Keats used it as a noun in his famous sonnet about discovery—

> Then felt I like some watcher of the skies
> When a new planet swims into his ken

—the word's meanings encompassed both range of vision and range of understanding. It distinguished for Keats the kind of seeing done by a true discoverer from that of men who merely look with casual curiosity or with wild surmise. (Anyone can stumble onto something new; a true discoverer perceives the significance of his discovery, knows that there is a new order in the world or in the heavens: not only are there maps of the new to be made, but all the old maps must be changed.) To name is to have known, and to know is to have seen.

Such, at any rate, is the fundamental premise that seems to run through all forms of phanopoeia, as if this power were continually engaged in the attempt to make real that lost clarity of vision for the language of poetry. The riddle, as a basic form of phanopoeia, derives from this same process of seeing, knowing, and naming. Although riddles are now just a game and even to folklorists a minor form of folk literature, traces of an older seriousness surround the riddles posed to Sophocles' Oedipus and Shakespeare's Pericles, for whom it was find the answer or lose your life. Poets, moreover, will still struggle with their namings as if their necks depended on it, and solve their puzzles with the same satisfaction of watching the Sphinx die of shame. Then, it may seem to the rest of us, they become sphinx-like in turn, masters in an old tradition who hide their meanings in obscure riddles and puzzling images. But the riddle is still a naming and a teaching, and in folklore or in poetic imagery the puzzle is meant ultimately to reveal rather than to conceal.

For many anonymous masters on this planet the riddle remains a vital poetic form, a way of charging language with meaning. If at one time it was felt that riddles were unknown to certain cultures, the extensive comparative work done by folklorists now shows that riddles occur in the oral traditions of all cultures and that riddle-making is a universal activity of the human mind, something we would expect if the riddle is truly a root of lyric poetry.[1] The riddle's sense of discovery, as well as its connection with poetic imagery, is easy to see in a Bantu riddle which asks for the name of "that which digs about in the deserted village" (the heart, which always turns to think of the past).[2] This riddle, however, is almost a lyric poem already, with a literary sentiment that goes beyond most folk riddles. The oldest riddles we have are from ancient Babylon, preserved in what was apparently a schoolbook (on a clay tablet, of course) which gives some riddles in Sumerian along with Assyrian translations. In spite of their great age they are more characteristic than the Bantu riddle of what is collected today from oral tradition:

> You went and took the enemy's property;
> the enemy came and took your property.

> Who becomes pregnant without conceiving,
> who becomes fat without eating?

The schoolbook does not give the answers to the riddles, and we hesitate over them puzzled, as the schoolboy must have done long ago, until he saw: a shuttle passing to and fro, and a rain cloud.[3]

The most important scholarly work on riddles has been done by Archer Taylor, whose *English Riddles from Oral Tradition* is a comparative collection drawing on hundreds of regional and national collections of riddles from all over the world. For Taylor, the structure of a riddle is based first of all on a description of one thing in terms of another thing: the familiar "Humpty Dumpty" riddle, for example, describes an egg in terms of a man. Such a riddle is essentially a comparison, and this fundamental characteristic of riddles is reflected in Taylor's method of classification which groups the riddles according to whether the object (the "answer") is compared, say, to a person, to several persons, to animals, to several animals, to plants, to things, or to a generalized living creature.

We can see such a comparison in a Vogul riddle which compares a group of fence posts, each with a cap of snow, to a group of peasant women: "Back of the village sit those who have donned white kerchiefs" (*ER*, p. 9). There is a clear image in this riddle, a strong sense of picture, and focusing on the structure of comparison rather than on just the answer shows that the riddle also contains all the essentials of a metaphor. It is a metaphor with one term concealed. This characteristic of riddles has been noticed often, and Aristotle commented in the *Rhetoric* that good riddles can provide us with good metaphors (*Rhet*. iii.2.1405b4-6). It can be seen as well in a Yakut riddle from Asia which compares a rainbow to a piece of multicolored silk hanging in the field:

In the field a piece of silk in five colors is becoming pale,
Neither you nor I can grasp it.[4]

The metaphorical comparison is slightly more complex in a lovely riddle from Sweden: "Father's scythe is hanging across mother's Sunday skirt" (the crescent moon).[5] The scythe is compared to the moon, the skirt is compared to the sky, and the relationship of the scythe and the skirt is compared to the relationship of the moon and the sky. This is the fullest form of a metaphor, and a lyric poet finding this might also see further relationships, drawing them into a poem involving husband and wife, times to work and times to rest, meanings of evening and home, or many other possibilities latent in the initial discovery of the riddle.

Another class of riddles is based not on a single metaphorical comparison but on a series of comparisons which enumerate the attributes of the hidden object. The sense of discovery is still at work, however, as the enumeration draws a circle of word pictures around the object. In some riddles of this kind a central image is found that unifies the individual comparisons; in others the individual comparisons are not at all related to each other. In a Dutch riddle for the human face, a series of comparisons leads to the central image of a street scene: "Two lanterns, two dirty allies, two files of soldiers, and a red huckster" (*ER*, p. 454; "allies" must certainly be "alleys"). A strange riddle from Ireland draws instead the central image of a melancholy countryside: "Two fences of stone, two pools of water, two human graves, and two [small] bunches of rushes" (teeth, eyes, nostrils, eyebrows).[6] Other riddles of this class, lacking any particularly strong sense of a central image, simply present a series of comparisons which point from their different directions in toward the object, or answer, at the center. A riddle from Iceland goes: "Who is the swift one that found me on the road? Neither the sun nor any other light shines on him. I have often seen him running alongside ships at sea. He needs no clothing or food, is visible to all but tangible by none" (shadow; *ER*, p. 662). Although the shadow is compared to a person, a generalized "he," the enumeration of comparisons does not build any particular central image that might bind his attributes together.

The riddles we have considered up to now are based primarily on image and metaphor; they are dominated, we might say, by a strong sense of picture. There are, however, many riddles which involve almost no sense of picture and which are instead based on a mental puzzle, a paradox. Aristotle was also aware of this "contradictive" characteristic of riddles (*Poet.* 22.1458a26-27), and folklorists refer to it as the "block element." The riddle "What grows smaller the more you add to it?" (a hole) carries only the vaguest sense of a picture and is structured primarily on a sense of paradox. A riddle, we remember, is a question that stops (or "blocks") us until the puzzle becomes clear and we find the answer. Purely "contradictive" riddles are also an accepted part of riddling tradition, and many of them are based on some kind of verbal paradox such as the word-play logic of this riddle from Oxfordshire: "What God has never seen, the king seldom sees, and we see every day" (an equal; *ER*, p. 680). At the bottom of many apparent paradoxes is often a pun, as in the riddle known throughout the United States, Canada, and the West Indies "Black and white and red all over" (a newspaper; *ER*, p. 624). A pun will usually limit a riddle to a particular language, of course, and the following riddles were all collected from the children of the British Isles:

> What runs but never walks?   (a river)
> What goes out without putting its coat on? (a fire)
> What turns without moving?   (milk)[7]

But there are many other ways for a paradox to arise in riddles. The Serbian riddle "A fire burns in the middle of the sea" (a lamp, or samovar) is based on a paradox arising from what appears to be a contradiction of the laws of nature (*ER*, p. 595).

Riddles, then, can work from either of two basic elements, the metaphorical presentation of an image or "picture" or the presentation of an intellectual paradox in which the sense of picture is slight or non-existent. The most familiar riddles, however, and those which are most interesting from our point of view, are those that combine both elements, fusing picture and thought. In riddles of this kind the implied metaphor or comparison is used to create the paradox, as in the Yakut riddle which first compares the rainbow to a piece of silk and then goes on to say that no one can grasp that piece of silk. The Serbian riddle for a lamp also contains a paradoxical image, a fire burning in water, and there is another one in the Irish riddle:

> A little lady sweeping the path
> Without a wisp [and] without a small bush.
>   (the wind; *IR*, p. 35)

A riddle for the moon shining on the water, also from Ireland, works in a similar way: "A white mare in the lake and she does not wet her foot" (*IR*, p. 14). The picture is given, and then the paradox; the complete riddle is a fusion of the two.

Different developments of this sense of the pictorial and the paradoxical can be seen in two forms of a riddle comparing snow to a bird:

> A milkwhite gull through the air flies down,
> And never a tree but he lights thereon.

In this form the riddle is based mainly on the metaphorical comparison, and the puzzle of a bird that lands on every tree is only slightly developed. A fuller form of what is probably the same riddle, however, shows in addition to the basic image a much more complicated sense of paradox:

> White bird featherless
> Flew from Paradise,
> Perched upon the castle wall;
> Up came Lord John landless,
> Took it up handless,
> And rode away horseless
> To the King's white hall.   (*ER*, p. 123)

In this version the imagery and the paradox are woven together through every line. The snow is a bird without feathers who flies from a land beyond flight, and the sun is a lord without land who can lift the bird without hands and ride away without a horse. The second version seems to represent a fuller fusion of image and puzzle, but only because it is more explicit. The process can be seen again in a similar riddle collected in the southern United States:

> She washed her hands in water
> Which neither fell nor run;
> She dried her hands on a towel
> Which was neither woven nor spun.
>
>   (dew and sun; *ER*, p. 463)

31

Here again imagery and paradox, the visual patterns and the intellectual patterns, work together to make us see.

We have, then, riddles in the form of a metaphorical image juxtaposing two objects or actions, riddles in the form of a simple verbal paradox, and riddles in a fuller form that combines elements of image and paradox into a unity.[8] I do not mean to suggest that the fuller form is a "truer" riddle than the simpler forms, for we also find in oral tradition enigmatic questions and puzzles without either element. But the fuller form shows us two important elements of poetry fused at the very roots of poetic language. If the riddle is in fact the root of phanopoeia in the language of lyric poetry, then this power involves more than just "a casting of images upon the visual imagination." The riddle asks a question: What is the *name* of water that neither falls nor runs? What is the *name* of a towel that was neither woven nor spun? In the process of finding the name, of reading the unknown in terms of the known, paradoxes arise because the unknown never completely fits into the known. The riddle is more than simply substituting one name for another. To name is to have known, and to know is to have seen—yet the sense of paradox is present even in the initial act of seeing and is never completely resolved. It is here, it seems, that the riddle as a root form of poetic imagery becomes most interesting to us, for the process of resolving the paradoxes implicit in the imagery becomes a way of knowing. This is true even in the riddles based on a simple comparison: in thinking of the moon and the sky in terms of father's scythe and mother's Sunday skirt, meanings of the scythe and the skirt, of father and mother, and even of the moon and the sky have expanded for us. In having seen, we have created a space for fuller knowing. What Aristotle said of metaphor applies as well to the riddle: it engenders thought by teaching us something (*Rhet.* iii.10.1410b10-15).

One thing that the riddle-root itself teaches us, then, is that poetic imagery in general is more than just "picture."

The comparison of a man to a tree is a common riddle that has also become a traditional poetic image. A Canadian riddle develops this comparison in both its pictorial and its paradoxical senses:

> In spring I am gay,
> In handsome array;
> In summer more clothing I wear;
> When colder it grows,
> I fling off my clothes;
> And in winter quite naked appear.

(a tree; ER, p. 215)

We can watch a poet, one well versed in paradox, opening a poem with this same basic comparison, but without explicitly working out the paradoxes held in the image:

> That time of year thou mayst in me behold
> When yellow leaves, or none, or few, do hang
> Upon those boughs which shake against the cold,
> Bare ruin'd choirs where late the sweet birds sang.

(Sonnet 73)

Yet the paradoxes are there. Time of year compares very well with time of life, cold with age, and the state of the tree with the state of the man, but none quite fits completely. The tree will come back green in the spring, but the man will not; like a fallen church or sacked monastery, his ruin is final. Unless, that is, (and here the image turns again) the spring resurrection in nature implies or promises a similar rebirth in man. This poem, I will suggest, cuts off that possibility, yet it is there in the space created by the image, a space for fuller definitions of the name "man."

Turning from the folk riddle itself to the riddle-root in poetic imagery, we first see two ways in which this root directly enters the language of complex poetry. Both ways lead to minor forms, as far as the history of poetry is concerned, but both forms offer important glimpses into the poet's language. The first form is simply the literary riddle, a more or less direct imitation of the folk riddle by a literate, educated writer. Galileo, Cervantes, Swift, and Heine were all attracted enough by riddles to write their own literary imitations. Literary riddles are, in their way, counterparts of literary imitations of folk ballads, and like "The Rime of the Ancient Mariner" or "La Belle Dame sans Merci" they usually carry unmistakable signs of sophisticated authorship which clearly set them apart from folk riddles. One such sign, seen frequently in literary riddles of the Middle Ages and the Renaissance, is the presence of an abstract theme or idea as one component (usually the hidden component) of the riddle. Folk riddles ask us to find concrete objects as answers; Tatwine, an eighth-century archbishop of Canterbury, wrote Latin riddles with answers such as philosophy, the four ways of interpreting a text, and the prepositions that govern two cases. Scaliger, the Renaissance critic, wrote riddles on the themes of God, necessity, nature, fate, and hope (LR, pp. 62, 74).

Even when a writer adopts an image from a folk riddle his consciously literary style tends to open out the riddle into a longer, more elaborate, and more involved form. Archer Taylor notes that the literary riddle often sacrifices the unity of a single comparison in favor of a wealth of details, frequently drawing together entirely different conceptions of the hidden object (LR, p. 3). This medieval Arabic riddle is a good example of the literary riddle, and it demonstrates the *embarras de richesses* that Taylor feels is characteristic of the form in general:

> What is that sea which is not of water, which increases and diminishes during the night, and in which one can neither leap nor drown;
> Which contains something in the shape of a serpent, a serpent having no hole to which to retreat and having a mouth in which, O my friend, there is a thing

That one sees—there is no mistake about it—whether
one is near or far, that hides itself daily in very truth
to reappear anew,
   That vanishes during the day, but spreads on human
faces the light of dawn as soon as night looks upon it,
   That watches like a lover whom love compels and
kills on hills and at the bottom of valleys?

(LR, pp. 20-21)

The answer is "a lamp," and we may recall for comparison
the simplicity of the Serbian folk riddle for a lamp: "A fire
burns in the middle of the sea." For another example, we
can compare an Irish folk riddle for the rainbow, "A
bridge on the lake without stick [and] without stone" (<i>IR</i>,
p. 41), with a treatment of the same image by Schiller:

> Von Perlen baut sich eine Brücke
> Hoch über einen grauen See,
> Sie baut sich auf im Augenblicke,
> Und schwindelnd steigt sie in die Höh'.

> A bridge forms from pearls
> High over a gray sea,
> It rises up in a moment,
> And dizzily soars aloft.

("Parabeln und Rätsel")

Schiller was more interested than the Arabic writer in catching the simplicity of a folk riddle, and in fact this first
stanza has also been found in oral tradition in Sweden.[9]
But he elaborated on the paradoxical characteristics of the
bridge for two more stanzas—the tallest ship can sail under
it, it cannot bear any load, it cannot be approached, it
comes and goes—and later composed another stanza ex-
plaining the answer ("sie heißt der Regenbogen").
   There is no reason, however, for holding up the folk
riddle as the goal of the literary riddle, and both the Arabic
riddle and Schiller's riddle become something quite at-

tractively different. In western Europe the earliest literary riddles in a vernacular language are the Old English riddles in the Exeter Book which, while they show their literary descent from medieval Latin riddles, also give us fine passages of their own dealing with such favorite Anglo-Saxon themes as the winter sea, arms and armor, mead, John Barleycorn, and the harp. The Anglo-Saxon sense of transience is nicely caught in the Old English riddle of a moth who eats words: the bookworm who swallows the noble songs, histories, and wise writings of men but is itself no wiser for it.[10] Although the literary riddle has always been a relatively minor form, the very existence of the form, with its invitation to involved elaborations of image and paradox, speaks for the strong attraction that the riddle-root holds for poets.

The riddle can also be seen making its initial steps into complex poetry through the kenning, a form which involves condensation rather than elaboration. This form too is seen at its best in the literature of the Middle Ages, and in particular in the language of Old Norse and Old English poetry. The kenning tightens the elements of a riddle into a figure of traditional formulaic diction: it presents a riddle in miniature. The word itself is cognate with Keats's "ken," and the Old Norse verb *kenna* holds all our meanings of seeing, knowing, naming, and teaching. The kenning, in short, is a name for an object based on a way of knowing it.

In his edition of *Beowulf* Fr. Klaeber used the designation "kenning" in a general sense for those compounds which refer to an object by some form of poetic periphrasis, such as *helmberend* ("helmet-bearer") for "warrior" or *beadoleoma* ("battle-light") for "sword."[11] Recently, however, scholars have found it necessary to make further distinctions, which in practice meant returning to the definitions already made by Snorri Sturluson in his medieval treatise on poetics *Skáldskaparmál*. Here we find that a figure referring to an object in terms of something that it *is* belongs to the class of *kend heiti*. The *helmberend*, for example, and the use of *hæðstapa* ("heath-stepper," *Beow.* 1368) for "stag," are *kend heiti*. A warrior *is* a helmet-wearer, and a stag *is* something that steps (more or less) along the heath. The kenning proper, on the other hand, refers to an object in terms of something that it *is not*. A sword is not a light, but it can be seen flashing in battle the way a torch flashes in the night, thus a *beadoleoma*. The distinctions are clear in theory, though, as we might expect, the practical boundaries are not sharp. A. G. Brodeur classes *swanrad* ("swan-road" or "riding-place of the swan," *Beow.* 200)—for the sea—as a *kent heiti*, and C. L. Wrenn states that it is a kenning.[12]

The distinction between kennings and *kend heiti* becomes more than an exercise in classification when we look at kennings with an eye for their riddle roots. "Who wears a helmet?" is not much of a riddle for "warrior," but "What is the light that flashes in battle?" could begin a fine riddle for a bright sword. Like a riddle, it sees the sword as something else, and also like a riddle it suggests a miniature puzzle to be solved. As Brodeur points out, the *kent heiti* is a familiar allusion and is not meant to puzzle the listener, but a kenning, on the other hand, "pleases only as a riddle pleases; it also contains an allusion or a comparison, but requires the listener to ferret out its secret through the exercise of his own ingenuity" (*The Art of Beowulf*, p. 249). Similar riddle puzzles are incipient in the kennings in *Beowulf* which see the sun as *heofones gim* ("heaven's gem," v. 2072) or *rodores candel* ("the sky's candle," v. 1572), the body as a *banhus* ("bone-house," v. 3147), and in the kenning in *Judith* which sees an arrow as a *hildenædre* ("battle-adder," v. 222). In each of these kennings, as in a riddle, an image generates a puzzle, a way of seeing that leads to a way of knowing. The arrow bites its victim with the deadly sting of a poisonous snake, and the concealment of one of these terms could produce either a riddle or a kenning. On this basis it might even be possible to suggest a resolution of the conflict above by pointing out that there are many folk riddles that compare the sea to a path or a road (*ER*, pp. 78-79), and that by analogy *swanrad* does indeed seem to be a true kenning.

The literary riddle and the kenning can be seen as early stages of the riddle-root's progress into the language of complex poetry. It may be more interesting from our point of view to observe the riddle as it appears in fully developed lyric poetry. Once the eye is aware of riddle roots it can spot them lying beneath many of the metaphors, images, paradoxes, and word plays of sophisticated and complex lyric poets. This is not meant to imply any historical assertion that knowledge of riddles "influenced" a poet's imagery, or any biological assertion that the poet grew an image from a particular riddle. It does suggest, however, that the riddle is the root of the lyric element in the sense that both the riddle maker and the lyric poet developed their respective expressions through the same associations of picture and thought, the same process of seeing, knowing, naming.

Shakespeare may not have heard any of the riddles occurring from Ireland to Mongolia that compare the sky to a cloth, yet his "morn in russet mantle clad" shows a mind making the same associations as the Swedish riddler who saw the evening sky as mother's Sunday skirt, or an Arabic riddler who saw the night sky as "A cloak with countless buttons, it cannot be folded or carried about" (*ER*, p. 520). Wordsworth's dancing daffodils spring from the same roots that produced many riddles comparing plants to dancers, as in this riddle from Maryland:

> Out in the garden
> I have a green spot,
> And twenty-four ladies dancing on that;
> Some in green gowns,
> And some in blue caps.
> You are a good scholar,
> If you riddle me that.   (flax; *ER*, p. 348)

A Lincolnshire riddle which compares the sun to a ubiqui-
tous person who seems to be engaged in a troublesome in-
vasion of privacy:

> Round and round the house
> And in my lady's chamber   (*ER*, p. 71)

shows some similarity to the opening conceit of Donne's
"Sunne Rising":

> Busie old foole, unruly Sunne,
> Why dost thou thus,
> Through windowes, and through curtaines call on us?

Donne may have known the riddle (a version of it was
recorded in his days), but it seems far more likely that he
was seeing the same thing and naming it anew in his lines.

At times a poet will stay so close to a riddle root that his
poem turns back into a literary riddle. A medieval lyric
from The Harley MS., known as "The Man in the Moon,"
opens with the image of a man who, because of his unique
situation, simultaneously "stands and strides"—a good riddle, involving both picture and paradox. A Wyatt poem develops from the initial image of a lady's gift a series of
riddle paradoxes:

> A ladye gave me a gyfte she had not
> And I receyvid her guifte I toke not.
> She gave it me willinglye, and yet she wold not,
> And I receyvid it, albeit I coulde not.
> If she geve it me, I force not;
> And, yf she take it agayne, she cares not.
> Conster what this is and tell not,
> Ffor I am fast sworne, I maye not.

There are folk parallels to this riddle, but perhaps the
closest analogue is a North Carolina literary riddle from an
early nineteenth-century almanac:

To her lover a lady said, "Give me, I pray,
What you have not, nor can have, but might give away!"
Let each hereafter his dullness repent,
The fool did not know 'twas a kiss that she meant.[13]

In the Wyatt poem a mental puzzle begins in a paradoxical image, generating a riddle-poem that seems to look both back to the medieval literary riddles and forward to the intricate images and verbal paradoxes of Elizabethan sonnets and metaphysical lyrics.

The seventeenth-century metaphysical style of poetry is particularly interesting for the ways it involves the riddle radical in greater complexities of imagery and paradox. When Samuel Johnson expressed in the "Life of Cowley" his well-known reservations concerning the metaphysical poets, he said that their ingenious form of wit depended on "a combination of dissimilar images, or discovery of occult resemblances in things apparently unlike." This shows a good feeling for riddles, though his next comment —"The most heterogeneous ideas are yoked by violence together"—misses the importance of the riddle or the metaphysical image as a discovery, a seeing into something in a manner that leads to a valid way of knowing. A traditional image found in many riddles discovers resemblances between the eyes and projectiles of various kinds, as in the Bantu riddle "The stones, the far-throwers" (Cole-Beuchat, p. 143) or in the Albanian riddle "Two arrows with black wings reach wherever they wish" (ER, p. 607). Crashaw worked with this same way of knowing something about the eyes:

> Eyes, that bestow
> Full quivers on loves Bow;
> Yet pay lesse Arrowes then they owe.
> ("Wishes. To his (supposed) Mistress")

Although Crashaw complicates the comparison by adding the conventional emblem of Love and his arrows, the basic discovery of the riddle is there, as it was in many other Renaissance and Baroque love poems.

Dr. Johnson's opinion of love poetry in the metaphysical style is also well known, particularly with reference to John Donne. Donne's offenses seem to lie at least partly in his own realization of how close his conceits are to riddles. He seems to have caught himself in the middle of a typical example in "Loves infinitenesse," recognizing that for him a poem about love is a poem about riddles:

> Loves riddles are, that though thy heart depart,
> It stayes at home, and thou with losing savest it.

His conceits often show tightly woven paradoxes arising from visual scenes, and we can see in them a complication of elements found in the riddle. Riddles that compare the human face to a landscape or a street scene become in "The good-morrow" a comparison of the face to a world:

> My face in thine eye, thine in mine appeares,
> And true plaine hearts doe in the faces rest,
> Where can we finde two better hemispheares
> Without sharpe North, without declining West?

This is of course a long way from a folk riddle, and Donne has doubled the puzzle by adding what is actually another riddle root: the eyes that can hold a world. ("Two little holes that refuse to be filled; there enter people, oxen, goats and other things," goes a Bantu riddle for the eyes— Cole-Beuchat, p. 141.) Yet the basic riddle pattern can be recognized: a comparison is made that discovers "occult resemblances" between two different things, paradoxes arise where the two overlapping meanings do not quite fit, and in that space Donne learns new meanings of his love, naming it a world "Without sharpe North, without declining West."

Even more complex is the discovery in Donne's "Hymne to God my God, in my sicknesse." It concerns not love but

death, and the vision of the entire poem grows out of a
riddle root established in the second stanza:

> Whilst my Physitians by their love are growne
> Cosmographers, and I their Mapp, who lie
> Flat on this bed, that by them may be showne
> That this is my South-west discoverie
> *Per fretum febris*, by these streights to die. . . .

A resemblance is discovered between the speaker's body,
flat on the bed, and a flat map. The doctors, with the riddle
of human sickness before them, read the body-map and see
the sickness lead through the south-west straits into the unknown regions of death. But then the riddle turns back
on itself, and in the next stanza the speaker, who as the
map is part of the riddle, makes the final discovery himself.
Having seen from maps that the extreme west touches the
east, he knows that his death will touch the resurrection.
The entire poem, in fact, is based on the theme of finding
a fuller knowledge through the structure of the body/map
riddle.

Donne of course raises the riddle radical to higher powers,
but that is what we expect a complex poet to do with roots.
Modern poets, as they explore beneath the rational and
logical forms of discursive language into the deeper structures of poetic language, often rediscover or re-create along
the way this fundamental radical of lyric. Like many other
modern poems, Robert Creeley's "My Love" is almost a
literary riddle, with the answer given in the title:

> It falleth like a stick.
> It lieth like air.
> It is wonderment and bewilderment,
>   to test true.
>
> It is no thing, but of two,
>   equal: as the mind turns to it,
> it doubleth,
>   as one alone.

> Where it is, there is
> everywhere, separate,
> yet few—as dew
> to night is.

There is no mistaking this for anything but a modern poem, but at the same time it reaches back—quite consciously, I think—to explorations of love's riddles similar to those made four centuries earlier by Wyatt. And the explorations made by Donne are recalled in another poem, "Song," in which Creeley develops darkly insoluble premonitions from this opening riddle:

> What I took in my hand
> grew in weight. You must
> understand it
> was not obscene.
>
> Night comes. We sleep.
> Then if you know what
> say it.
> Don't pretend.

This time there is no answer given.

In the last version of her poem "Snow," Emily Dickinson used an image we have already seen in riddles, the snow/bird:

> It scatters like the Birds—
> Condenses like a Flock—
>
> *(Poems,* No. 311)

Dylan Thomas reaches beneath the prose logic of similes in his poem "Because the Pleasure-Bird Whistles" to give us a playful turn on the same basic structure in the image of a snowstorm as "a wind that plucked a goose." Emily Dickinson's poetry has already been fruitfully studied as a development of riddle forms by Dolores Dyer Lucas in *Emily Dickinson and Riddle* (DeKalb, Ill.: Northern Illinois Univ. Press, 1969), and a similar study of the riddles at the

roots of Thomas' poetry would also find much to say. The
face/landscape comparison of the riddles appears once
again in Thomas' "Where Once the Waters of Your Face,"
a poem that sees the dry bed of a sea-channel as the face of
a lost love:

> Where once the waters of your face
> Spun to my screws, your dry ghost blows. . . .

The "heron / Priested shore" of his "Poem in October"
and the "prayer wheeling moon" of "In Country Sleep" are
other tight images that verge on the riddle or the kenning.
The first could easily be turned back into a riddle asking
"Who are the priests bowing on the shore . . . ?" and if
prayer wheels had been a part of Germanic religion "heav-
en's prayer wheel" might easily have become a kenning in
Beowulf. Again, Thomas is a poet who makes more than
riddles, and these roots are only parts of his complex lyric
poems, yet it is basically the same eye that sees snow-ker-
chiefs on the fence posts, rainbow bridges in the air, and
star buttons in the cloak of the sky that sees, when looking
at a flock of birds rising above a hillside:

> a black cap of jack-
> Daws Sir John's just hill dons.
>
> ("Over Sir John's Hill")

If the riddle is, as I suggested, a naming, it is a form of
naming that calls upon a particular power of the language
of poetry. It is a naming that creates a space rather than
reduces it. Even at the roots phanopoeia is more than just a
sense of the pictorial in poetry. The riddle's peculiar vision
leads to complex and paradoxical ways of knowing something, ways that good poets will not allow to be resolved
simply. The developed complexities of Shakespeare and
Donne, or of Emily Dickinson, Dylan Thomas, and Robert
Creeley, are not likely to be found in all levels of poetry,
but the root forms of these complexities often will be.
An image that occurs in many riddles sees a candle as a
man. A common form of the riddle is:

Little Nancy Etticoat
In a white petticoat
And a red nose;
The longer she stands,
The shorter she grows.   (*ER*, p. 222)

The riddle is built on both picture and paradox, and the
answer, "a white candle," creates a simple juxtaposition in
the mind: candle/man (well, woman). A more complicated
riddle from Spain makes the same juxtaposition, but the
burning of the candle, a simple contradictive element in the
first riddle, is now seen in terms of a man's life: "I was
created on the mountain and I came to my end at the
altar" (a candle). (Archer Taylor's explication of this riddle. "The reference to the mountain signifies the bees making wax out of doors. . . . 'I came to my end at the altar'
signifies the burning of the candle, and at the same time
aptly describes the end that any mortal might expect"—
ER, p. 429.)

It is not far at all, radically, from these riddles to a
simple lyric like Cavafy's "Candles":

Days to come stand in front of us
like a row of burning candles—
golden, warm, and vivid candles.

Days past fall behind us,
a gloomy line of burnt-out candles;
the nearest are still smoking,
cold, melted, and bent.

I don't want to look at them: their shape saddens me,
and it saddens me to remember their original light.
I look ahead at my burning candles.

I don't want to turn, don't want to see, terrified,
how quickly that dark line gets longer,
how quickly one more dead candle joins another.[14]

Cavafy's image begins by comparing candles to days, but he

45

very quickly comes upon the basic form that compares a burning candle to a man's life.

We have already looked at the tree/man image in the opening quatrain of Shakespeare's Sonnet 73. The last quatrain of the same poem brings in a riddle root very like the burning candle; it sees the life of man as a dying fire:

> In me thou seest the glowing of such fire
> That on the ashes of his youth doth lie,
> As the death-bed whereon it must expire,
> Consum'd with that which it was nourish'd by.

The image here is more explicit about its own paradoxical character than Cavafy's candle image as Shakespeare sees the fire being quenched by the ashes of its fuel. It completes an important progression in the poem, moreover, by leading up to a deeper knowing concerning a man's life: unlike the autumn of the first quatrain or the fading twilight of the second quatrain, the dying fire of this last quatrain is an irreversible process. The fire will not come back, and neither, the speaker has learned, will the aging man.

Other poets have developed this same root into their own ways of knowing. Wallace Stevens saw the candle not as an image of the life of man but as an image of the brief life of man's imagination in "Valley Candle," and Dylan Thomas in "Light Breaks Where No Sun Shines" riddled the mystery of life's genesis with his image of "a candle in the thighs." Perhaps the richest development of this root appears not in a lyric poem at all, but as the "flaming minister" that lights Othello's way to murder Desdemona: "Put out the light, and then put out the light." What is there seen and known and named creates a space too large to enter into now, but we can observe how the humble riddle repays our interest by leading us through the center of poetry.

III. EMBLEM

PoETs exploring the strongly visual power of phanopoeia in the language of poetry periodically experiment with introducing an actual picture into a verbal context as an effectively direct way of casting images upon the visual imagination. The most sustained development of such an experiment came in the emblem books of the sixteenth and seventeenth centuries. The emblem books very literally forced sculpture or painting into words by presenting the phanopoeic sense of picture through an actual engraving or woodcut. Words and picture worked together, with the picture, in effect, part of the language of the emblem. The full form of the riddle, we saw, is essentially a metaphor with one element concealed; similarly, it is possible to see the emblem as a metaphor existing in a dual medium. Even without the presence of an actual picture, however, the emblem method is a special case of phanopoeia, a particular way by which this power of poetic language moves from seeing to knowing. The metaphorical images of folk riddles tend to bring together concrete elements such as snow and a bird, the rainbow and a bridge, or the teeth and two stone fences. Riddles linking a concrete object and an abstract concept betray themselves as literary compositions: their roots are in the inkhorn (to use their own habit of mixing metaphors) rather than in oral tradition. This linking of the concrete and the abstract, however, is the method in which the emblem excels, and there is no difficulty at all in finding good emblems on subjects such as God, necessity, hope, or love.

The classical tradition had taught that art mediates between history and philosophy by uniting the example and the precept. Like Sidney, the emblematists respected and followed this view of art, and, again like Sidney, they conceived of the union of example and precept as serving a moral purpose. The emblem, like the riddle and the kenning, is a teaching. Just as the paradoxes that arise from bringing together concrete images in the riddle ultimately teach us something, so is the linking of a concrete picture with a moral meaning in the emblem meant to teach us something. The sense of paradoxical thought at the roots of phanopoeia in the riddle becomes manifest in the emblem as a more explicit and more self-conscious didacticism. The method is one that has been out of fashion for a while in serious literature, but it is one with a long history, and a taste for it reaches from at least as far back as the Bible up through the Alexandrian period and the Middle Ages to the actual emblem books of the Renaissance and Baroque periods.

The flourishing emblem-book tradition reached England from the Continent in about the middle of the sixteenth century, though there was a deep interest in English letters for emblems, *imprese*, and heraldic devices long before that. The first major emblem book in English was Geoffrey Whitney's *Choice of Emblemes*, published by Plantin in Leyden in 1586.[1] In an age of vigorous and fruitful plagiarism, Whitney made free use of plates from Continental emblematists, particularly Alciati, that were available from Plantin, but his verses were in English. The culmination of the tradition in England came with the emblem books of Francis Quarles, whose *Emblems, Divine and Moral* (1635) was the most popular of the English emblem books.[2] The emblematists were erudite and somewhat pedantic Renaissance men, and they displayed these qualities liberally in their books, yet the books themselves were popular literature. They appealed to a much wider audience than did the metaphysical poetry of the same period, and though they often started with the same visual image the emblems rarely attempted the complexities of phanopoeia reached by Herbert or Donne.[3]

The emblem, like the riddle, takes many forms, but it is possible to see a basic theory growing out of the many experiments. The emblem book as it was developed in England usually consisted of three elements: the plate itself, which gave the pictorial element in an engraving or woodcut; the printed verses, which explored the themes presented in the plate; and the "moral" or motto, which was a line or two in the style of, and often an actual quotation from, a traditional epigram, literary proverb, or moralistic *sententia*. In addition to these three elements there were usually added on before or after the verses two or three short Biblical quotations or homiletic lines from Fathers of the Church such as Augustine or Ambrose, but these additions were incidental to the basic structure.

The picture was not meant to be simply an illustration for the verses. It was less a "natural" or representational image than an older, more stylized form of visual representation based on the symbolic language of iconology. Similarly, the verses were not simply a verbal description of the picture: they were not, in the best examples, what Jean Hagstrum has defined as "iconic" poetry—poetry that, like Homer's passage on the shield of Achilles or Keats's "Ode on a Grecian Urn," is based on a real or imaginary work of graphic art.[4] Both the picture and the verses were meant to work in their own unique ways toward completing the emblem as a whole. The third element, the motto, was kept separate from the verses, and the emblematists felt that it should also be in a foreign language (Greek and Latin were particularly favored). There were many emblem books in which these distinctions were not kept or even attempted, books in which the picture was no more than an illustration for the verses or the verses simply a point-by-point interpretation of the picture. In the most interesting examples of the emblem method, however, the three-part form was respected: the plate gave the visual image, the verses explored in their own way some of the conceptual meanings of the image, and the motto pointed the way toward some general resolution of the visual and the verbal expressions.

The emblem writers recognized that their method involved a linking of picture and thought, of the sensuous and the intellectual. These writers of the sixteenth and seventeenth centuries were fascinated by the Egyptian hieroglyphic in much the same way that the poets of the twentieth century have been fascinated by the Chinese ideogram, though there seems to have been no Ezra Pound among the emblematists who put forth a theory of poetry and meaning based on character-writing. There was, nevertheless, a feeling that the emblem derived from the hieroglyphic in the sense that the picture held contained within itself a meaning that was to be "read." Geoffrey Whitney, in the sixteenth century, felt that the emblem was like the decorative devices used since classical times to show forth some meaning. He defined the emblem in a literal sense (from the Greek verb ἐμβάλλεσθαι) as a work of inlay, a decorative ornament set in or on a surface: "properlie ment by suche figures, or workes, as are wroughte in plate, or in stones in the pavementes, or on the waules, or suche like, for the adorning of the place: havinge some wittie devise expressed with cunning woorkemanship, something obscure to be perceived at the first, whereby, when with further consideration it is understood, it maie the greater delighte the beholder" ("To the Reader," *A Choice of Emblemes*). Beginning with the visual element, Whitney sees the picture as involving meanings which, like riddles, are at first "somethinge obscure." When the obscurity is solved, the picture is still there before us, not left behind but enriched.

In the seventeenth century Francis Quarles defined the emblem with more emphasis on the meaning behind the picture, but he too held to the fusion of image and thought in the emblem:

AN EMBLEM is but a silent parable: let not the tender eye check, to see the allusion to our blessed SAVIOUR figured in these types. In holy scripture he is sometimes called a sower, sometimes a fisher, sometimes a physician; and why not presented so, as well to the eye as to the ear? Before the knowledge of letters, GOD was known by Hieroglyphics. And indeed what are the heavens, the earth, nay, every creature, but Hieroglyphics and Emblems of his glory?

("To the Reader," *Emblems*)

The fusion of picture and thought, of the concrete and the abstract, or (emphasizing the moral meanings) of example and precept: this is the heart of the emblem method. In her study *English Emblem Books*, Rosemary Freeman writes that two distinct ancestors, one pictorial and one intellectual, contributed to this fusion. The hieroglyphic stands behind the pictorial elements of the emblem; the moralistic and sententious elements can be traced back to the rhetorical concerns of the epigram:

In all contemporary criticism, emblems are connected, explicitly or implicitly, with two main interests, interest in decoration and interest in rhetoric. From the very beginning it had been uncertain whether the form derived from Egyptian hieroglyphics or from the Greek anthology, whether, that is, its pictorial or its rhetorical side was of prime importance. This doubt resulted in a dual classification: emblems were associated by some critics, notably Abraham Fraunce, with insignia, arms, symbols and hieroglyphics, and by others, for instance by John Hoskins in his *Directions for Speech and Style* with allegories, similitudes, fables and poets' tales. The dichotomy is of course false, for the whole essence of the emblem method is that in it picture and word are intimately combined; but the two sides do none the less exist, though they exist in conjunction and not independently of one another. . . .   (pp. 85-86)

The two sides exist, we might add, in the ancestors themselves, in the Renaissance understanding of Egyptian hieroglyphics as images used by Egyptian priests to foreshadow
divine ideas, and in the origin of the epigram as verses
engraved on a work of art such as a statue, monument, or
funerary stele.[5] The dual nature of the emblem, moreover,
with hieroglyphic on the one hand and rhetoric or verbal
wit on the other, can be seen as corresponding to the union
of image and verbal puzzle in the riddle. The whole principle of emblem writing, Miss Freeman says, is "the equating
of pictorial detail with moral ideas" (p. 60). The riddle's
tight paradoxes become in the emblem didactic parables,
with the paradoxes partly resolved on a general level by
the motto, and the process of seeing and knowing becomes
the special case of linking the concrete with the abstract.

Two emblems from Whitney will serve as examples of
this principle. In the first, he used one of the most popular
plates of emblem literature, a picture of a human figure
whose one arm is winged and raised toward the sky and
whose other arm is pulled down by a weight.[6] His picture
presents a man standing on a hilltop, striving to reach the
glorious skies above him. The man is looking upward, one
foot raised and one foot on the ground; his winged left arm
is reaching up, but his right arm is tied to a heavy stone
which pulls it downward. Above him in the distant clouds
birds fly freely. The verses develop the theme of a similar
condition in all those soaring spirits who, wishing for ex-
cellence, fame, or high estate, are held down by the re-
straints and cares of poverty:

> I shewe theire state, whose witte, and learninge, ofte
> Excell, and woulde to highe estate aspire:
>> But povertie, with heavie clogge of care,
>> Still pulles them downe, when they ascending are.

The motto is a general statement of the same theme: *Paupertatem summis ingeniis obesse ne provehantur* ("Poverty

Paupertatem summis ingeniis obesse ne prouehantur.

Ad Doctiss. virum Dn. W. MALIM.

O N E hande with winges, woulde flie vnto the starres,
   And raise mee vp to winne immortall fame:
But my desire, necessitie still barres,
   And in the duste doth burie vp my name:
That hande woulde flie, th'other still is bounde,
With heauie stones, which houldes it to the ground.

My wishe, and will, are still to mounte alofte,
   My wante, and woe, denie me my desire:
I shewe theire state, whose witte, and learninge, ofte
   Excell, and woulde to highe estate aspire:
But pouertie, with heauie clogge of care,
Still pulles them downe, whan they ascending are.

Iuuenalis.—

*Haud facilè emergunt, quorum virtutibus obstas
Res angusta domi, &c.*

Pro bono

In fœcunditatem, sibiipsi damnosam.

I F fence I had, my owne estate to knowe,
   Before all trees, my selfe hath cause to crie:
In euerie hedge, and common waye, I growe,
   Where, I am made a praye, to passers by:
And when, they see my nuttes are ripe, and browne,
My bowghes are broke, my leaues are beaten doune.

Thus euerie yeare, when I doe yeelde increase,
   My proper fruicte, my ruine doth procure:
If fruictlesse I, then had I growen in peace,
Oh barrennes, of all most happie, sure
   Which woordes with griefe, did A G R I P P I N A grone,
And mothers more, whose children made them mone.

Alciatus.
*Quid fronti prosit com-
mentary..*

Sueton. in vita
Neronis.

Locus è nare
Ouidiana.

*Cernit ego se nunquam peperissem , tristior essem:
Ista Clytemnestra digna querela fuit.*

Otiosi

Homo homini lupus.

Sicut Rex in imagi-
ne sua honoratur:
sic Deus in homine
diligitur, & colitur.
Non est pulchrum
orendere, qui deni
amat. nec poteſt
minorem odiſſe. Chryſ.
super Matth. 11.

Mira fabula de Ar-
ionde & Leone.
Aul. Gellii. 1. ca. 14.

Idem de Arione
lib. 16. cap 19.

NO mortall foe so full of poysoned spite,
  As man, to man, when mischiefe he pretendes:
The monsters huge, as diuers authors write,
  Yea Lions wilde, and fishes weare his friendes:
And when their deathe, by friendes suppos'd was fought,
They kindnesse shew'd, and them from daunger brought.

ARION lo, who gained store of goulde,
  In countries farre: with harpe, and pleasant voice:
Did shipping take, and to CORINTHVS woulde,
  And to his wishe, of pilottes made his choise:
Who rob'd the man, and threwe him to the sea,
A Dolphin, lo, did beare him safe awaie.

Virxú poëticum.

Quis nescit veras olim delphina per vndas,
  Lesbia cum ſacro vata tuliſſe lyram?

To Ca-

Hierog. !

Sine Lumine inane.

How canst thou thus be useful to the Sight?
What is the Taper not indu'd with Light?

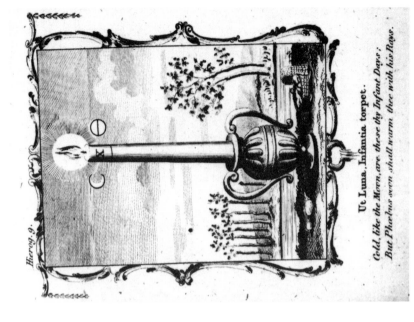

Hierog. 9.

Ut Luna. Infantia torpet.

Cold, like the Moon, are these thy Infant Days;
But Phœbus soon shall warm thee with his Rays.

Hierog. 6.

Tempus erit.

The Time shall come when all must yield their Breath;
Till then, Time checks th'uplifted Hand of Death.

Ut Sol ardore virili.

Now like the Sun, He glows with manly Fire;
Invokes the Muse, and strikes the Thracian Lyre.

DEUTERONOMY xxxiii. 25.

As thy days, so shall thy strength be.

The poſt
Of ſwift-foot time
Hath now at length begun
The kalends of our middle ſtage :
The number'd ſteps that we have gone, do ſhow
The number of thoſe ſteps we are to go :
The buds and bloſſoms of our age
Are blown, decay'd, and gone,
And all our prime
Is loſt :
And what we boaſt too much, we have leaſt cauſe to
[boaſt.

Ah me !
There is no reſt :
Our time is always fleeing.
What rein can curb our headſtrong hours ?
They poſt away : they paſs we know not how :
Our Now is gone, before we can ſay now :
Time paſt and future's none of ours :
That hath as yet no being ;
And this hath ceas'd
To be :
What is, is only ours : how ſhort a time have we !

And

Hierop 12.

Ut Sol ardore virili.

Now like the Sun, He glows with manly Fire,
Invokes the Muse, and strikes the Thracian Lyre.

Hierog. 15.

Plumbeus in Terram.

The Sun now sets; all hopes of Life are fled;
And to the Earth We sink like Weights of Lead.

Hierog. 14.

Invidiosa Senectus.

Envious Old Age obscures thy feeble Light;
And gives Thee Warning of approaching Night.

Qui me alit me extinguit.

E v e n as the waxe dothe feede, and quenche the flame,
So, loue giues life; and loue, dispaire doth giue:
The godlie loue, doth louers croune with fame:
The wicked loue, in shame dothe make them liue.
    Then leaue to loue, or loue as reason will,
    For, louers lewde doe vainlie languishe still.

A CHOICE
OF EMBLEMES,
AND OTHER DEVISES,

For the moſte parte gathered out of ſundrie writers,
Engliſhed and Moralized.

AND DIVERS NEWLY DEVISED,
by Geffrey Whitney.

A worke adorned with varietie of matter, both pleaſant and profitable: wherein thoſe that pleaſe, maye ſinde to fit their fancies: Bicauſe herein, by the
office of the eie, and the eare, the minde maye reape dooble delighte throu-
ghe holſome preceptes, ſhadowed with pleaſant deuiſes : both fit for the
vertuous, to their incoraging: and for the wicked , for their admoniſhing
and amendment.

To the Reader.

Peruſe with heede, then frendlie iudge, and blaming raſhe refraine :
So maiſt thou reade vnto thy good, and ſhalt requite my paine.

Imprinted at LEYDEN,
In the houſe of Chriſtopher Plantyn,
by Francis Raphelengius.
M. D. LXXXVI.

hinders the highest genius from gaining promotion"—p.
152). The theme of the verses is simple and pragmatic, but
the emblem as a whole, through the linking of the man
who wants to fly with the man of learning held down by
the gravity of human exigencies, takes a cliché and opens
it out to a wider contemplation of the conflicts between
desire and necessity.

The second emblem from Whitney involves its image
with a meaning even more explicitly. The picture shows a
tree laden with nuts, and men breaking the branches of the
tree as they beat down the nuts with heavy sticks. In the
verses the tree itself speaks, developing the paradox that
its good fortune in bringing forth desirable fruits has lead
directly to its bad fortune:

> Thus everie yeare, when I doe yeelde increase,
> My proper fruicte, my ruine doth procure:
> If fruictlesse I, then had I growen in peace,
> Oh barrennes, of all most happie, sure
> Which wordes with griefe, did AGRIPPINA grone,
> And mothers more, whose children made them mone.

Again the motto is a statement of the general concept toward which the picture and the verses work: *In fœcunditatem, sibi ipsi damnosam* ("On fruitfulness injurious to its
own self"—p. 174). Starting with the image of the flailed
tree, the emblem develops in the verses some of the meanings of this image (as well as adding the further image of a
mother whose children brought her tragedy), and then in
the motto gives a general, sententious statement that sum-
marizes the movement from example to precept.

The emblem of one winged arm and one weighted arm,
showing the conflict of desire and necessity, and the emblem
of the fruitful tree being damaged for its fruit, showing how
good fortune can cause bad fortune, are forms of metaphor
met at the level of popular literature. Here they are embodied in the dual medium of the emblem book. At the

same time the joining of the concrete and the abstract in the emblem is a special case of metaphor. There is an emblem in Quarles in which the picture shows a shipwrecked girl struggling through the waters to shore. The verses develop the theme of the soul alienated from God (Bk. III, Emb. XI, pp. 133-35). The emblem is basically a metaphorical comparison juxtaposing two elements: one element, the more concrete one, exists in the visual medium; the other element, a more abstract one, exists in the verbal medium. The third element, the motto, is essentially an act of literary criticism directed toward the metaphor: it is supplied by a reference to Psalms 69:15 ("Let not the waterflood overflow me, neither let the deep swallow me up, and let not the pit shut her mouth upon me") and suggests a general area in which the two elements of the metaphor come together. Both the visual and the verbal elements of the metaphor are necessary, for the emblem depends on the relationship set up between them, on seeing a fusion of two terms which yields the metaphorical comparison "a shipwrecked girl is like an alienated soul." By concealing the second term we could produce a riddle—though not a very good one, for this joining of the concrete and the abstract is the special domain of the emblem method.

Although the emblem method is seen most clearly in the dual medium of the emblem books, imagery that joins a concrete picture to an abstract concept is of course an old and familiar way of seeing, knowing, and naming. Set an emblem in motion and what do you get? The journey of a Piers Ploughman, a quest by a Red Crosse Knight, a pilgrim's progress. Although the emblem books were not full allegories in the sense of being sustained narrative tales, the emblem writers inevitably found themselves writing miniature allegories, for allegory is a larger form based on the same kind of involvement of picture and meaning. The shipwreck emblem in Quarles includes verses of assembly-line allegory of this nature:

54

The world's a sea; my flesh a ship that's mann'd
With lab'ring thoughts, and steer'd by reason's hand:
My heart's the seaman's card, whereby she sails;
My loose affections are the greater sails:
The top-sail is my fancy; and the gusts,
That fill these wanton sheets, are worldly lusts.
Pray'r is the cable, at whose end appears
The anchor hope, ne'er slipp'd but in our fears:
My will's th' unconstant pilot, that commands
The stagg'ring keel; my sins are like the sands. . . .

The ship allegory has old roots in medieval literature, and
it is still with us in political rhetoric and in sermon literature as the ship of state and the ship of life. (Ishmael in
Moby-Dick had an eager taste for emblems and allegory,
and as he waited in Father Mapple's chapel for the sermon
to begin he read the emblem of the prow-shaped pulpit:
"Yes, the world's a ship on its passage out, and not a voy-
age complete; and the pulpit is its prow.")

Rosemary Freeman shows that John Bunyan, experienced
preacher that he was, would often turn his allegorical images into riddles with the intention of producing more
strongly a sense of questioning thought in his readers. *The
Pilgrim's Progress* asks questions such as "Why doth the
Fire Fasten upon the Candle-wick?" "Why doth the Pelican
pierce her own Breast with her Bill?" or "What may one
learn by hearing the Cock to Crow?" These questions are
all pietistic emblems posing as riddles. "All, presented
slightly differently," Miss Freeman comments, "could constitute emblems. The intellectual stimulus that such riddles,
and the emblems among them, could provide is evident
from the frequency and length with which they are em-
ployed in *The Pilgrim's Progress*" (*English Emblem Books*,
p. 221). They are of course literary riddles, and the "intellectual stimulus" they provide is that particular form of
phanopoeia mastered by the emblem method. Yet it con-

55

tinues to be a reading of the unknown in terms of the
known: in having seen the concrete picture (shipwrecked
girl) we come to know something about the abstract concept (alienated soul). We have, so to speak, found a name
for the condition of alienation and have created a space
for fuller knowing about that condition.

Allegory, Marxist critics say in attacking it, is a "dehis-
toricized" form, a concept that brings us to a power of
phanopoeia we have as yet considered only implicitly. In
addition to the concern for imagery and a sense of thought,
and also as a result of this concern, phanopoeia can be seen
forcing poetry into a "spatial" consciousness, one in which
the time elements of poetry—movement, sequence, progression—are frozen or obliterated. Introducing a sense of the
pictorial into a verbal medium, Jean Hagstrum writes,
"necessarily involves the reduction of motion to stasis or
something suggesting such a reduction. It need not elimi-
nate motion entirely, but the motion allowed to remain
must be viewed against the basic motionlessness of the arrangement" (*The Sister Arts*, p. xxii). We can see in the
emblem books how the time elements of poetry are held
static, how the temporal connections between the con-
stituent parts of the emblem are evaporated, and how there
is in general a sense of caught time which later reappears
in modern poetry as the "timeless moment" of the Image.
This takes us somewhat beyond the fundamental structures
of the language of lyric into the larger question of spatial
and temporal form in literature in general, but any discussion of phanopoeia is constantly flirting with this old
critical problem, and the emblem in particular openly in-
vites it.

The strong tendency of some poetry toward visual imagery and spatial pattern has always generated discussions
relating poetry to the visual arts of painting and sculpture,
arts in which temporal form usually has no place. Aristotle
appears to have discouraged this relationship by limiting

opsis to the representations presented by the actors and the stage settings; he commented that of the six elements of tragedy, this one is least connected with the art of poetry (*Poet.* 6.1450b16-20). Other classical critics, however, linked poetry and the visual arts in ways which later prompted many serious inquiries into the relationships between these arts. The usual starting points for these discussions are two: a phrase, attributed by Plutarch to Simonides of Ceos, that painting is silent poetry and poetry is a speaking painting,[7] and a phrase from Horace's "Art of Poetry": *ut pictura poesis* (*Ars poetica* 361). They are only slight hints, particularly the latter in which Horace, discussing flaws in poetry, says only that "poetry is like painting" in that some poems appear at their best when viewed from a distance, while other poems are most pleasing when they are examined closely. But implications of these phrases expanded far beyond their original contexts as they were carried through Renaissance criticism. The famous Horatian phrase is part of the actual titles of many emblem books, and the phrase from Simonides obviously stands behind Quarles' definition of the emblem as "a silent parable." Even after the decline of emblem books a concern for poetry as a speaking picture is seen reflected in the many richly detailed landscapes and framed "prospect views" of eighteenth-century poetry.[8]

Poetry faces certain limits, however, in trying to bring a sense of the pictorial and the idea of space into language, and the best-known discussion of these limits is Lessing's *Laocoon* (1766), his attempt to separate the arts of poetry and painting or sculpture once and for all. For Lessing, poetry was essentially a temporal art, like music, and painting and sculpture were essentially spatial arts. He saw any attempt to mix a temporal art and a spatial art as a confusion of basic principles that inevitably led to a second-rate product. A poetic image, he pointed out, is not a material picture but a creation in language, and language is a medium that imitates action, not space. It is this view of language that is the central hypothesis underlying Lessing's conclusions: "If it be true that painting employs wholly different signs or means of imitation from poetry,—the one using forms and colors in space, the other articulate sounds in time,—and if signs must unquestionably stand in convenient relation with the thing signified, then signs arranged side by side can represent only objects existing side by side, or whose parts so exist, while consecutive signs can express only objects which succeed each other, or whose parts succeed each other, in time."[9] The "convenient relation" between the medium of imitation and the object of imitation is the vulnerable heel of Lessing's hypothesis. It clearly derives from the classical doctrine of art as mimesis, but an overly literal and reductive view of that doctrine; the language of poetry (and the language of painting as well) is probably more independent and also more complex than Lessing assumed. (Similar assumptions had led earlier to the "unities" of time and place as rules for the art of drama, and the year before *Laocoon* was published Samuel Johnson had still found it necessary to explain in his *Preface to Shakespeare* that mimetic art should not be confused with verisimilitude: "Imitations produce pain or pleasure, not because they are mistaken for realities, but because they bring realities to mind.") Leo Spitzer writing on medieval lyrics, G. Wilson Knight on Shakespeare, Jean Hagstrum on neoclassical poetry, and Joseph Frank on modern poetry and fiction all testify that Lessing's argument contradicts an important dimension of literary experience.[10] It may not be accurate in every case to call that dimension "spatial form," but the term does apply quite literally to the emblem method.

Lessing's concepts of spatial and temporal form probably are more useful adapted to our coordinates for analysis than as absolute distinctions between the arts. Poetry, it seems to me, lies finally not on either axis but somewhere between the two, yet it is obvious that certain modes of poetic language will approach much closer to one axis than the other. The emblem emphasizes visual imagery and spatial form, an emphasis that remains a strong power of the emblem method even without the presence of an actual picture. Yet, although the emblem method derives primarily from phano-poeia, we can see Lessing's time elements of poetry existing within the spatial form. Even the pictures in the emblem books could themselves incorporate the temporal dimension within their spatial frames. An artist who wished to make a picture based on a narrative, and who also wished to make his picture conform to Lessing's version of the unity of time, would have to choose a single dramatic moment from the narrative and limit his representation to that one moment in time. An emblem artist, however, had available to him older resources in the language of visual representation. In Whitney's *Choice of Emblemes* we see an emblem on the theme of "man is a wolf to man" (p. 144). The picture is based on the story of Arion, and it shows both Arion being thrown overboard by treacherous mariners who covet his gold and Arion riding safely away on the back of the rescuing dolphin—a kinder friend to man, the verses explain, than are his fellow men. As Rosemary Freeman points out, the unity of time was not a matter of concern for this artist or for the emblem artists in general: "The emblem writers had no such rule of consistency; often several events which could not by any chance have sub-sisted together in one time are found side by side within the single frame of an emblem from Wither or Whitney. The encroachments of the painter upon the domain of the poet occur everywhere in the emblem books. Whitney's Arion, for example, is cast into the waves and is seen simultaneously riding away upon the dolphin in another corner of the picture" (*English Emblem Books*, p. 12).

The emblematist was dealing with a story, a narrative, and therefore with time. Unlike the artist concerned with the limitations of spatial form, however, the "encroachments of the painter upon the domain of the poet" allowed him to introduce events from separate times into his picture and gave him a way to present the meaning of an entire narrative within a pictorial form. The sequential events of the narrative are presented simultaneously in the spatial pattern, and time, rather than flowing, is held frozen in the picture. Arion falling into the waves and then riding away on the dolphin can just as easily be seen in the reverse sequence, or in no sequence at all, since both events are simultaneously present to the viewer. Presented in this way, both events work as elements of the meaning of the picture and of the complete emblem: spatial pattern becomes conceptual pattern as the meaning is understood outside of the sequence of the Arion story.

In the Arion emblem, the picture itself catches time in a simultaneous spatial pattern. On a different level, the emblem as a whole—picture, verses, and motto—also works toward catching time in the spatial and conceptual patterns of the visual imagination. The emblem method's involvement with spatial and temporal form is seen perhaps at its best in Francis Quarles' *Hieroglyphics of the Life of Man,* his second emblem book. Shorter than other emblem books, it has a unity of conception that most of the other books did not attempt. The book consists of fifteen emblems built on an image we have already met, the comparison of a burning candle to the life of man. Each picture centers on the state of the candle, and the verses take up meanings involved in the basic metaphor. The picture of the first emblem, for example, shows a tall, unlit candle, its base set in an urn and its wick reaching up into dark clouds. The motto is *Sine Lumine inane* ("Without light, it is useless"). The candle sits in a darkened landscape, with a dark city in the background and clouds obscuring the sky (Hier. i, pp. 245-47). The next emblem shows the hand of God reaching from the clouds to give light to the candle, now set in a spring landscape beside a flowing river (Hier. ii, pp. 248-50). Succeeding emblems show the winds endangering the new flame, a physician causing the flame to burn too quickly by trimming it, and an angel with a shield guarding the flame from the winds.

The sixth emblem is particularly interesting. Death, pictured as a skeleton, holds an arrow and a candle snuffer. He is about to extinguish the flame, but Time, represented as the bearded man with an hourglass, restrains Death's arm. The verses are a debate between Death and Time. Death is the prince of darkness who hates the flame and wants to extinguish it immediately, but Time tells him that he must wait for the appointed hour: "What need'st thou snatch at noon, what will be thine at night?" The motto, *Tempus erit* ("There shall be a time"), and the line from Ecclesiastes heading the verses, "To every thing there is an appointed time," express the same meaning at a more general level. The picture, by showing Time holding back Death, shows that the hour has not come, but the verses stress the certainty that it will come, and back in the picture we see a sundial on which the shadow, we know, is moving steadily forward (Hier. VI, pp. 260-62).

The handling of time in this emblem and in the other emblems of *Hieroglyphics of the Life of Man* makes this small book an unusual achievement in emblem literature. Throughout the book time is treated both thematically, as part of the moral meaning, and technically, as part of the emblem method. In each emblem Quarles respected his dual medium: the picture freezes time by presenting different elements in a nonsequential pattern in the manner of Whitney's Arion, whereas the verses emphasize time, especially the passing of time and the transience of human life.

The last seven emblems in the book deal with the seven ages of the life of man as the candle in the pictures burns down through seven stages marked off on its side. In the picture for the first stage, the infancy of a man's life, the candle stands in pre-dawn darkness; a baby-basket lies on the ground beside it and behind it stand trees in early bud. The verses develop the idea that the first ten years of life are a virtual loss, not really life at all: "we rather breathe than live" (Hier. IX, pp. 269-71). In the next emblem, the candle stands in a spring landscape just beginning to blossom, and the sun—which in the verses becomes the "light of reason"—is just appearing. In the fields behind the candle a young boy is being thrown from a vigorous horse, which in the verses becomes two things. It is first the "proud-neck'd steed" of life which the impetuous youth, disdaining his tutor, wants to command by himself, but by the end of the verses it has become a reminder that time itself is running away, carrying youth into age: "Time's headstrong horse / Will post away" (Hier. x, pp. 272-74).

The flame becomes brighter as the candle burns down into maturity, and other elements in the pictures, such as the trees, the flowers, the seasons, and the time of day, change accordingly. Different cycles—the life of man, the burning of a candle, the turning seasons, the life of a tree, the rise and fall of cities—are superimposed in the pictures in a way that obliterates linear, historical time and points instead to a conceptual state. In the fourth age of a man's life the flame is brightest of all and the motto reads *Ut Sol ardore virili* ("As the sun with manly ardor"). An oak tree is bearing acorns, generating the next cycle in its strength, while a lyre rests against a laurel tree, suggesting that this is the age in which poets bear their richest fruits. It is a day of fullness, but again the verses emphasize transience and passing time:

> The post
> Of swift-foot time
> Hath now at length begun
> The kalends of our middle stage:
> The number'd steps that we have gone, do show
> The number of those steps we are to go:
> The buds and blossoms of our age
> Are blown, decay'd, and gone,
> And all our prime
> Is lost:
> And what we boast too much, we have least cause to boast.
> (Hier. xii, pp. 278-80)

(In this emblem, we see, the poet has encroached upon the domain of the painter and given us a shaped poem, balanced until the last line and its premonitions of time running out.)

In the sixth stage, traditionally called post-maturity or senescence, the shortened candle stands with dimming flame in an autumn landscape. A tree's fruits lie rotting on the ground while Death, again pictured as a skeleton, shakes down the leaves. The verses begin in the manner of Gray's Elegy with people returning home from their labors as the day grows old, and they then go on to describe a season of "cold autumnal dews" and the ills that passing time will bring to a man in this age: falling hair, care, envy, spite (Hier. xiv, pp. 284-86). In the last stage, senility, the candle is a dim stub almost completely burned down into its urn. The landscape is probably late November: there is a dead tree stump in the foreground, a group of ruined buildings in the middle-ground, and the sun setting behind the hills. In no pictorial ground, but standing on either side of the candle, are a kingfisher and the astrological sign of cold, melancholy Saturn, the governor of old age. The same sign is the alchemical symbol for lead, and the emblem's motto is *Plumbeus in Terram* ("Like lead, into the earth he falls"). The verses follow such examples of rise and decline as the sun, the candle, a man, and a castle which was once great and strong enough to protect its builders from enemies but now lies in ruins protecting no one (Hier. xv, pp. 287-89).

In each emblem, then, time is very much present, but its basic nature of sequence is changed by the emblem method. Time is always moving from past to future in the verses, but in the pictures the sequence is broken as elements are presented in simultaneous spatial pattern. The effect of the emblem as a whole is one of further spatialization, but something much fuller than simply a reduction of motion to stasis. The verses and the picture together create a metaphorical relationship that lifts the emblem out of time into a conceptual space that contains both the visual images of the picture and the moving time of the verses. Here the verses and the picture meet in the motto, a *mot* that mediates between them by naming on a general, conceptual level meanings arising from the basic metaphor that compares the candle to the changing life of man. The emblem method turns out to be a more complex form than Lessing imagined either for painting or for poetry, for temporal form exists in the emblems, but it is always within the spatial pattern set up by image and concept. It was in this sense of caught time, worked out in the emblem books, that the richest possibilities of *ut pictura poesis* ultimately lay.

The sense of an image or picture, the sense of intellectual patterning, and the sense of time caught in space form a complex which lies at the roots of lyric poetry. We have called that complex phanopoeia and we have seen in the emblem tradition a somewhat fuller development of those elements which were found in root form in the riddle. The ways in which this complex works in more sophisticated forms of lyric poetry are the subjects of the following two chapters, but we might note here that the emblem, like the riddle, often turns up in such poetry in its simple form, a case of the root showing above ground. The imagery of much Renaissance and Baroque poetry frequently shows the emblematic union of a concrete picture and an abstract concept, and many of the complex images of Spenser, Sidney, Jonson, and Shakespeare have plainer sisters in the emblem books. A picture of a torch turned upside down and the motto *Qui me alit me extinguit* ("Who nourishes me, extinguishes me") appears in Whitney's *Choice of Emblemes* as an emblem for love (p. 183), and so it is used in Shakespeare's *Pericles* as the device presented by the Fourth Knight (II.ii.32-35). (The similar image in Sonnet 73, however, the dying fire "Consum'd with that which it was nourish'd by," is less an emblem than a way of knowing that belongs to the riddle root.) Crashaw's penitent weeper, whose eyes are two fountains, two "compendious oceans" of tears, used to be regarded as an infamous example of Baroque extravagance, but the same image had appeared earlier with no fuss in Quarles' *Emblems* as an actual picture of a woman sitting before a fountain with rivers of tears flowing from her eyes:

> O! that mine Eyes, like Fountains, would begin
> To stream with Tears proportion'd to my Sin.[11]

George Herbert especially tended toward emblematic expression in his poetry, and, just as poets write literary riddles with the answer given in the title, many poems in *The Temple*—"The Church-floore," "The Windows," "The Collar," "The Pulley," "Artillerie"—may be read as emblems with the title taking the place of the picture.[12] John Donne's conceits are generally more complex, with more of a sense of paradox and involved thought, than the moralizing images of the emblem books, yet the wreath of hair in "The Funerall" begins, at least, as an emblem for the spinal cord of the spirit. The compasses in "A Valediction: Forbidding Mourning," one of his most famous images, serve as an emblem for constancy. The same emblem, as Rosemary Freeman has shown, appears in George Wither's *Collection of Emblemes* (1635), also as an emblem for constancy; moreover, the same emblem had been used as a device by the Plantin press, and books published by Plantin, including Whitney's sixteenth-century *Choice of Emblemes*, had long carried the compass emblem and the motto *Labore et Constantia* on their title pages (*English Emblem Books*, pp. 146-47).

After the seventeenth century there was a general turning away in English poetry from the emblem's way of seeing, with its iconographic designs created primarily to be "read" for their meanings, toward more naturalistic and humanistic forms of imagery. Real landscapes and real human figures underlie the pictorial tableaux and allegorical personifications of eighteenth-century poetry, and, though the em-

blematic image never completely dies out, by the time of
the Romantics there are few firm compasses of constancy
left in the language of poetry. Instead of the grim skeleton
of Death with its long scythe we have Wordsworth's "Solitary Reaper," a Highland girl cutting grain in a "Vale
profound" and singing "As if her song could have no ending" of "old, unhappy, far-off things, / And battles long
ago" or of "Some natural sorrow, loss, or pain, / That has
been, and may be again." Instead of an autumn landscape
dominated by a candle burning down into an urn, with
Death shaking the leaves from a tree and with emblematic
hourglasses, sundials, ruins, or kingfishers scattered about,
we learn about the passing of time in Keats by seeing a
natural autumn landscape with human laborers at the end
of a harvest and English swallows gathering to depart.

But there is of course Blake, whose engraved plates joining visual picture and poetic text can be seen as taking the
emblem method, after a long period during which it had
declined into mere book illustration, to a final development
of its powers. Blake aimed, as one commentator writes, at
overcoming through the methods of his art the dualistic
view of a world separated into space and time: "his poetry
exists to invalidate the idea of objective time, his painting
to invalidate the idea of objective space. To state this posi-
tively, his poetry affirms the power of the human imagination to create and organize time in its own image, and his
painting affirms the centrality of the human body as the
structural principle of space."[13] The powers of Blake's
imagination reached far beyond those of the emblem writers, and ordering space according to the Human Form Divine was not the emblematists' way of seeing. Yet the fusion
of a dual medium into one complete art and the transformation of space and time through that art into a more
complex conceptual space marked out in the human imagination had been tried before, and perhaps briefly accom-
plished in the small emblem book *Hieroglyphics of the Life
of Man.*

IV. IMAGE

A CENTRAL CONCERN of modern poetry and poetics has been to re-explore and redefine the ideas of *ut pictura poesis*. The effects of phanopoeia in the language of poetry—the sense of an image or picture, the sense of intellectual patterning, and the sense of time caught in space—dominate some of the most interesting poetry of the modern period, and the kinds of things that we have seen happening in basic forms of phanopoeia, the riddle and the emblem, are seen again in the more complex forms of modern poetry. They are, in fact, often formulated as imperatives for that poetry. Ezra Pound and William Carlos Williams are two modern poets who particularly claim our attention here. They continue to be perhaps the most influential voices of modern poetry, and the subjects of active and controversial literary criticism, but they are important to us because they are poets who worked close to the roots. In poem after poem, and again in the critical essays, personal accounts, and provisional manifestos which make up a poet's thoughts on his art, both Pound and Williams show a deep preoccupation with the powers of phanopoeia and with what those powers can do in poetry. In addition, Pound does us a further service by directing us toward Japanese and Chinese poetry as carefully refined, and particularly illuminating, uses of those powers. The forms of phanopoeia in modern poetry involve us to some extent in a poetics of the visual imagination, an area in which there has already been much critical discussion and almost too much of nomenclature and categories, but our own concerns remain simple, limited as they have been all along to seeing and identifying the roots of lyric.

The visual emphasis of phanopoeia has been a part of

modern poetry from its beginnings. For the poetry that we
are presently interested in those beginnings are in London
in the period 1908-1914, in the new movement that soon
came to be called "Imagism." T. E. Hulme was an early
member of that movement, and he thought it heralded a
new form of classicism in poetry. He anticipated a dry, hard,
severely finite form of verse in which the poet would be the
counterpart of the new "classical" artist in painting and
sculpture—an artist in language carefully working to "get
the exact curve of what he sees whether it be an object or
an idea in the mind." The "great aim" of such poetry, he
said, "is accurate, precise and definite description," and its
visually precise language "always endeavours to arrest you,
and to make you continuously see a physical thing, to pre-
vent you gliding through an abstract process."[1] Ezra Pound
set forth three principles for the new poet to follow, the
first of which was: "Direct treatment of the 'thing,' whether
subjective or objective." Pound's famous demonstration of
that new poetry was the short poem which, he has already
told us, began with a vision of faces in a metro station and
the "sudden emotion" he experienced on seeing them:

In a Station of the Metro

The apparition of these faces in the crowd;
Petals on a wet, black bough.[2]

Phrases such as "direct treatment of the 'thing' " and "the
exact curve of what he sees" emphasize a poetic language
based on clear, precise seeing, a power of phanopoeia; for
if this power in the language of poetry is associated with
the assumption that to know is to have seen, then clear
knowing requires first of all that the eye see clearly.

But just what is seen, and what is known, in a poem
such as "In a Station of the Metro"? Although Hulme
called for "accurate, precise and definite description," the
poem obviously does not give an accurate description of the
scene in the metro station, and the image of petals on a wet,

black bough must have been seen somewhere else entirely. Pound, in another well-known dictum, said that such a poem does not "describe" anything; it presents. The entire "Metro" poem, in fact, is an example of what he defined as an "Image"—"that which presents an intellectual and emotional complex in an instant of time." The language he found to express his experience, Pound said, was a language of "pattern," and rather than a verbal description of the single scene the poem presents a juxtaposition of two images, the faces in a crowd and petals on a bough. What is seen by the poet, and presented by the poem, is not a painter's "view" but a structure of overlapping forms, and it is toward that structure that the visual precision is directed. "The 'one image poem,'" Pound wrote concerning this same poem, "is a form of super-position, that is to say, it is one idea set on top of another." As for what is known in this poem: "In a poem of this sort one is trying to record the precise instant when a thing outward and objective transforms itself, or darts into a thing inward and subjective."[3] The complete structure, the seen complex of faces and petals, transforms itself and darts inward, and the language of the poem attempts to catch both the precision of that seeing and the sudden emotion of that knowing.

Now all this, we notice, is a good account of what happens in a riddle. The full structure of the riddle is also a "complex" in which two objects or actions are seen juxtaposed, and in which, since the two elements are not identical, paradoxes and puzzles arise where one element does not fit the other. In attempting to resolve the paradoxes implicit in the imagery, meanings of both elements expand for us and the riddle becomes a way of knowing. Pound's poem, like a riddle, is not simply a pictorial description but a discovery, a way of seeing that leads to a new way of knowing. The emblem, though a special case of phanopoeia, also follows the same principles: the complete emblem is not simply the visual picture but a juxtaposition of picture, verses, and motto, with the picture only one element of a three-part structure. The emblematic juxtaposition of a concrete picture and a moral meaning is not a riddle's or a modern poem's way of seeing and knowing, but we have seen that it too involves complexities of phanopoeia that cannot be resolved simply.

The two lines of "In a Station of the Metro" took him more than a year (on and off) to compose, Pound said, and when he finally found a way to write the poem it was with the help of a form from Japanese poetry, the haiku. The model that he used for what he called the "*hokku*-like sentence" of his finished poem was a haiku attributed to Moritake (1472-1549):

> A fallen flower
> Returning to the branch?
> It was a butterfly.[4]

For us as well this Japanese poem and others like it are good models for understanding the forms of phanopoeia in the language of modern poetry. As Earl Miner has shown, these short poems from Japan strongly influenced modern poetic theory and practice, first by teaching the early Imagist poets to value a concise style, precise imagery, and the avoidance of didactic moralizing in their poems, and then by demonstrating clearly an important structural principle of poetry, the "form of super-position" which Pound borrowed from haiku and continued to use as a basic method in his own work long after "In a Station of the Metro."[5] Hugh Kenner has discussed fully how important these insights have been for Pound's poetry and for modern poetry in general—particularly the realization that certain poetic modes of statement work through structures of juxtaposition, and that "juxtaposed objects render one another intelligible without conceptual interposition."[6] Of course French Symbolist poetry and classical Greek lyrics were also strong influences for the Imagists, but haiku seem to show the phanopoeic structures of juxtaposition at their clearest. Since Pound has pointed to haiku as the roots of his own form, we will look briefly at a few of these Japanese poems to see what he and other modern poets have seen there. As we discuss the phanopoeic structures in haiku and in modern poems, the reader is asked to tolerate sympathetically the melodrama of the capitalized "Image," which is used to distinguish this verbal "complex" from the usual literary sense of "image," the "single image" or verbal description of a sense impression.[7]

The Imagist poets read Japanese haiku first in French and then in English translations. We know now that haiku are not "Imagist" poems and that in general these early views of Japanese poetry were somewhat limited. Along with clear, precise imagery, haiku use a full range of ways to charge language with meaning, including versification, diction, literary allusion, ambiguity, and word play. The poetry, moreover, is deeply associated with Eastern philosophical and poetic traditions. But it is the concreteness of the imagery, and the bare structure of the Image, that come across in translations. What those translations show is that a sharply focused Image can stand at the center of a poem, and it can stand there without further explanation or commentary: the Image identifies itself. The coming of night is frequently seen in poetry as a way of knowing about endings, especially when thoughts of man's mortality give a sober coloring to the clouds that gather round the setting sun. A poem by Issa (1763-1827) does not need to tell us that we are seeing something quite different from this as it juxtaposes two visual images, and two contrasting movements, in a moment shortly after the sun has set:

> The spring day closes,
> Lingering
> Where there is water.
>
> (*Haiku*, II, 38)

Seen clearly here is the light that remains high in the sky reflecting in pools of water which stand out against the darker landscape after sunset. What is known is something about spring—something involving pools of water left by spring rains and the light lingering in those pools, reflecting from a sky where that light is staying with us a little longer each spring evening. If the day closes, and its waning brings thoughts of endings, this small poem also sees a larger, and contrary, movement—the waxing season of spring—that lingers.

The phanopoeic sense of picture is strong in this poetry, but it is not picture poetry. A poem by Taigi (1709-1772) presents, without any visual images, a "super-position" made up of the senses of touch and hearing—

> Morning cold;
> The voices of travellers
> Leaving the inn.
>
> (*Haiku*, iv, viii)

—and which nevertheless sees a moment of morning clarity, a fresh start, and perhaps also a cold touch of loneliness and a feeling of being left behind. In a poem by Shōha (?-1771) the coming of spring is presented through two juxtaposed actions—

> Spring begins
> Quietly,
> From the stork's one pace.
>
> (*Haiku*, ii, 32)

—and the brief moment in which one action is seen against another contains a world. Although the stork has traditional associations in Japanese poetry with longevity and the New Year, which began in spring, the Western reader of this English translation probably would not see them. He does however see the stork as it could be seen, let us say, by any farmer or fisherman who throughout the winter had come out each morning and looked on the empty brown grasses of the river shallows. But this morning the stork is back, fishing with slow, deliberate steps in the shallow water, and the precisely focused poem somehow manages to contain the immense movement of one season into another season within the microcosm of one quiet pace.

The visual clarity of phanopoeia is there in haiku, but picture is not enough. This poetry is not description, and the things it presents are not snapshots of picturesque scenes. As in the riddle, the power of phanopoeia is in these poems directed primarily toward seeing—through the juxtaposition of objects, images, ideas, or anything else—some fundamental structure of overlapping forms. Each poem, moreover, sees and presents more than just one thing set on top of another thing; each poem is a "complex" that contains not one but several levels of juxtaposition. Moritake's haiku juxtaposes a blossom and a butterfly, a falling motion and a rising motion, a dying and a resurrection. Issa's poem juxtaposes the gathering darkness and a gathering of light, a waning day and a waxing season, a closing and a lingering. Taigi brings together a sound of voices and a feeling of cold, the touch of fresh hope and the touch of sad loneliness, a leaving and a remaining. Shōha brings together the small, quiet movement of the stork's one pace and the huge, quiet movement of the world turning toward spring. Pound's "Metro" poem is, we see now, rather than a simple juxtaposition of two things, a similar complex which also involves further levels of juxtaposition. The poem sees faces in a subway crowd set against petals on a wet, black bough, and this composition, Hugh Kenner has suggested, brings with it a rich set of other juxtapositions: the world of machines and the world of growing nature, ghostly apparitions in a dark underworld and life in wet, spring daylight, Persephone and Odysseus and Orpheus on earth and in Hades.[8]

The same principles are seen at work in other early poems written by Pound as he experimented with the structure of the Image, the "intellectual and emotional complex" presented in an instant of time:

Pagani's, November 8

Suddenly discovering in the eyes of the very beautiful
  Normande cocotte
The eyes of the very learned British Museum assistant.

Two people, the two components of the poem's Image, intersect in the eyes. Although they appear to be very different types of people, the juxtaposition brought about
by their eyes discovers further intersections. With sudden
surprise we see that however impulsive and openly carefree
the eyes of the Normande cocotte may appear to be, they
are subtle, discerning, and disciplined; at the same time,
we see that the educated and analytical museum assistant
has an impulsive eagerness and love daily renewed for
the old prints and drawings in the British Museum.

Another Image poem by Pound is "Alba":

As cool as the pale wet leaves
of lily-of-the-valley
She lay beside me in the dawn.

The Image of this poem is not simply the description of
the leaves, and not the remembered view of the woman at
dawn, but again the points where the two come together
and cross. They are brought together first of all by the
grammar of a simile, "As cool as," which makes explicit a
crossing at "cool." Other crossings are made, however, not
by grammar but by the structure of the Image. There is a
visual crossing in "pale," the pale wet leaves and the woman
seen in the colorless dawn light. She was cool and pale
like fresh new leaves, or perhaps she was "pallid, chill, and
drear" like Madeline's waking vision of Porphyro in the
colorless moonlight of "The Eve of St. Agnes"—both possibilities are contained in the Image. Other juxtapositions
in the complex presented by this poem come from the
courtly love situation implied by the title which, like the
titles of Robert Creeley's riddle poems and George Herbert's
emblematic poems, is here an integral part of the struc-

74

ture. The light that revealed the woman to the eyes of her lover was the dawn light that also signaled that they must separate. Although the love was probably adulterous, the image of the woman is seen together with the image of the fresh leaves, and perhaps the white flowers as well, of lily of the valley. The lines describe only coolness, but the Image presents far richer meanings.

As one more example of what phanopoeia's power of seeing illuminates in short Image poems, we have the slightly more involved structure of William Carlos Williams' "El Hombre":

> It's a strange courage
> you give me ancient star:
>
> Shine alone in the sunrise
> toward which you lend no part![9]

The visual sense of precisely seen imagery is strong in Williams' poetry, as it is in the haiku and the short poems by Pound, but what is primarily seen in "El Hombre" is again a structure, a juxtaposition of images, actions, and ideas. A star is seen against a sunrise, but the Image of the poem also contains the juxtapositions of something ancient and something new, and of a giving and a not-giving. The sunrise gives light and a new day; the star gives nothing toward that light, but it gives the speaker something that the sunrise cannot give. For a moment, perhaps, the poem seems to contradict its own statement, for the "strange courage" is given to the speaker, we see, not by the image of the star only but by the complex of an ancient star in a new sunrise. But then we see that there is a further level of juxtaposition in the poem as well, one which includes as part of the Image the speaker himself seen as someone who seems to accept what the star is giving and to reject what the sunrise continues to give nevertheless.

Among such paradoxes we can turn to ask what is known through this way of seeing. The visual precision in haiku and in the short Image poems by Pound and Williams obviously does not consist in nailing down the intellectual and emotional possibilities of the complex. There is something like an uncertainty principle at work here: the more precise the poetic Image, the less we can limit with prose definitions the meanings and emotions involved in it. We said that the riddle ultimately reveals rather than conceals, that through its paradoxes and puzzling contradictions it opens a space for fuller knowing about the things it sees. Similarly, the meanings and emotions of an Image poem are paradoxical ways of knowing held in the structure of the Image. The Pound poems are simple examples, yet like the riddle they open up spaces for fuller knowing— about metro riders underground and petals in the wet light, about a Normande cocotte and a British Museum assistant, about the pale, fresh leaves of lily of the valley and a mistress seen at dawn. Williams' "El Hombre" works in the same way to open up spaces about the sunrise, "el hombre" the star, and "el hombre" the man. The Image discovers, but does not describe, these things. It is a seen structure that, as Pound said, darts inward, a constellation that brings to the reader vision, apprehension, thought.

The Image that generates this process must of course be "significant," capable of becoming a sign to the hombre who sees it. Once again haiku clearly show basic forms of this power of phanopoeia and are good models for how it works in modern Image poems:

> Lying with arms and legs outstretched,
> How cool,—
> How lonely!   (Issa; *Haiku*, IV, xxv)

A bed on which one can stretch out and be cool is also a cool bed in which one can be lonely. Issa's Image of lying cool and lying lonely sees a paradox which darts inward, a matrix of vision and thought: something about freedom is known. A poem by Buson adds a haiku version to the candle/man root seen earlier in the riddles and emblems:

Lighting one candle
With another candle;
An evening of spring.

(*Haiku*, II, 55)

In English translation this haiku is in every way a poem
of the Image, discovering meaning through an Image
which juxtaposes a spring evening with the passing on of
the light. There is actually a double juxtaposition here,
for we see again a waning day and a waxing season, and set
against this we see a candle that has been burning and a
fresh candle being lit. At a point of complex intersections
is the action of passing on the light, and though the poem
does not say that this moment is a way of knowing about
the life of man, those ideas are among the meanings that
are seen in the space created by this Image.

Lying comfortably alone in bed or lighting one candle
from another candle is a fairly insignificant act until it is
caught and seen in a certain poetic structure. In both poems that structure involves some sense of contradiction and
paradox, and these are signs of their riddle roots: a riddle
is not simply the "answer" but the process, a way of seeing
that creates a space for fuller knowing. Among the historical and philosophical roots of haiku we find the Zen
kōan, an extreme form of riddle developed as a teaching
device by Zen masters sometime about the eleventh century
and later applied systematically in the Rinzai school of
Zen by Hakuin (1685-1768). "What is the sound of one
hand clapping?" Hakuin asked his disciples, and writers on
Zen tell us that this sort of question will remain trivial or
obscure until it transforms itself, darting inward and teaching the disciple a new way of seeing. A process similar to
this seems to be demanded by those haiku whose Images
at first seem meaningless or baffling to us—and then suddenly do not. In modern Image poetry this mode of thought
is again a sign of phanopoeia and the riddle root. From the
Image must come the insight, and explanations of it are

difficult, for the structure of the Image acts as its own language. Modern poets who have attempted to explain how the language of their poetry works tend to insist on the "anti-intellectual" nature of the Image, and to stress that modern poetry is concerned only with the precisely seen Image and not with ideas: "The image is not an idea" (Pound); "No ideas / but in things" (Williams). But "idea," the pedant will not resist saying, is the Greek second aorist infinitive ἰδεῖν ("to see"), and to know is to have seen. The Image is anti-intellectual only when the capacities of the intellect are limited to the logic and syntax of descriptive statements. The insights presented by a riddle, a haiku, or an Image poem are no less a language of ideas, a language structured by its own logic and syntax. "Images in verse," Hulme wrote, "are not mere decoration, but the very essence of an intuitive language" (*Speculations*, p. 135), and for Pound the Image was "the word beyond formulated language" (*Gaudier-Brzeska*, p. 88). Hart Crane wanted the entire poem to be a new word added to the reader's language of thought: "It is as though a poem gave the reader as he left it a single, new *word*, never before spoken and impossible to actually enunciate, but self-evident as an active principle in the reader's consciousness henceforward."[10]

Such a word, it is clear, is an "idea": something seen and known and named in the poem. "When we name it, life exists," Williams wrote. "The only means [the artist] has to give value to life is to recognise it with the imagination and name it; this is so. To repeat and repeat the thing without naming it is only to dull the sense and results in frustration."[11] Thus, in our last example from Japanese haiku, the poet Ryōta sees a moment seen often before, but names it anew in the structure of the poem:

> They spoke no word.
> The visitor, the host,
> And the white chrysanthemum.

> (*Haiku*, i, 192)

The configuration in Ryōta's Image of a flower which is silent and two people who choose not to speak names a complex of perceptions, experiences, and emotions. It is an "idea," a way of seeing that has darted inward, or, as Hart Crane said, a word "never before spoken and impossible to actually enunciate, but self-evident as an active principle in the reader's consciousness henceforward." The Image, like the riddle, the kenning, and the emblem, is thus also a teaching, an active principle that remains with us. After all the helpful work of the New Criticism, Image poems are not, finally, self-contained heterocosms but are *utile* as well as *dolce*. True naming is not arbitrary, not a giving of names but the discovery of names, as Ryōta sees the significance of one silent moment, knows it, and by naming it with his poem causes it to exist for us centuries after the moment of a guest, a host, and a white chrysanthemum has flickered away.

The discovery of names through the paradoxical structures of riddles, and the naming of complex spaces of human experience in the structures of Images, remain forms of phanopoeia, a power of the visual imagination. The same power organizes the structures of emblems, and involves those structures in concepts of *ut pictura poesis*. The introduction of a strongly pictorial power into a verbal medium seems necessarily to involve, as Jean Hagstrum said, "the reduction of motion to stasis or something suggesting such a reduction." We saw in the emblem books, however, that even poetry which not only seems to be but is sculpture or painting forcing itself into words need not be a still-life, a *nature morte*. The sense of the kinetic is not lost in the emblem method, but caught and held in the spatial and conceptual patterns of the visual imagination. The temporal dimensions of poetry—movement, progression, change—are still there, but *seen* in phanopoeic pattern. We next examine two further aspects of this way of organizing the language of poetry, and both show that the

Image also incorporates time and action by transforming them into complex forms of phanopoeia. The first is the poem of the "moving Image," which concentrates on introducing a sense of the kinetic into the basic Image structure itself. The second, closely related to the emblem method of Quarles' *Hieroglyphics*, emphasizes the sense of time and action caught in the "timeless moment" of the Image.

"The defect of earlier imagist propaganda," Pound, the chief early propagandist, wrote some twenty years later, "was not in misstatement but in incomplete statement. The diluters took the handiest and easiest meaning, and thought only of the STATIONARY image. If you can't think of imagism or phanopoeia as including the moving image, you will have to make a really needless division of fixed image and praxis or action."[12] The fine points of the various statements by poets on the "moving Image"—and on what Pound also called the "Vortex," and Charles Olson later called the "space-tensions" and "field" of the poem—belong to literary history. In general, those statements emphasize dynamic forces in the Image; the Image continues to be a spatial conception, but seen as a spatial pattern of energies and movements that is in some way analogous to the "vortex" of fluid mechanics or to an electromagnetic "field." As soon as objects (or images, or actions, or ideas) are placed side by side a relationship has been created, and forces are set up among the juxtaposed elements. We see throughout modern poetry that one basic assumption of the "moving Image" is that the juxtaposition of various elements in the structure of the Image generates forces in just this way. Pound's short Image poems are again primary forms, juxtapositions which set up tensions and energies between petals in wet sunlight and human faces out of the sun, between a very beautiful French woman and a very learned British Museum assistant, between dawn light that allows a lover to see his mistress and dawn light that sends her back to her husband.

The energy of relations, however, is not necessarily motion, at least not in poetry or in painting and sculpture. In Pound's "Return" we see a somewhat different way of catching time and action within a phanopoeic form:

> See, they return; ah, see the tentative
> > Movements, and the slow feet,
> > > The trouble in the pace and the uncertain
> > Wavering!
>
> See, they return, one, and by one,
> With fear, as half-awakened;
> As if the snow should hesitate
> And murmur in the wind,
> > and half turn back;
> These were the "Wing'd-with-Awe,"
> > Inviolable.
>
> Gods of the wingèd shoe!
> With them the silver hounds,
> > sniffing the trace of air!
>
> Haie! Haie!
> > These were the swift to harry;
> These the keen-scented;
> These were the souls of blood.
>
> Slow on the leash,
> > pallid the leash-men!

"It exists primarily in and for itself," Hugh Kenner wrote of this poem, "a lovely object, a fragment of Greek frieze, the *peripeteia* of impalpable huntsmen too firmly-drawn to be wraiths in a dream. . . ."[13] The poem is not, however, a description of a work of art, and not a simple interpretation of *ut pictura poesis*. There is a rhetoric: a visual imperative ("See . . ."), a speaker and audience implied, and thus a dramatic situation implied as well. Furthermore, images from the past occur in the poem ("These were . . ."), giving, at first, the illusion of narration. Yet beneath these are the basic principles of the Image, with the dramatic situation and the illusion of narration caught up in the forms of phanopoeia. The Image is created, as we now expect, through a set of juxtapositions, a structure of images, actions, and states of experience seen together. The turning back (Pound is using the word "return" primarily, though not exclusively, with this old meaning) of the troubled hunters is seen against the hesitation and reversal of the snow, "souls of blood" against "pallid the leash-men," and an earlier state of confident inviolability (" 'Wing'd-with-Awe,' " "Gods of the wingèd shoe") against the present state of uncertainty and fear ("the slow feet, / The trouble in the pace and the uncertain / Wavering!"). The images from the past are brought into the pattern of the present and the initial impression of narration is dissolved into that pattern; the final effect is in fact one of dynamic stasis. Except for the vaguely classical associations of the rhythms and diction, Pound gives no provenance for this poem, but cuts it free from geography and history. Who these figures are and what they have seen are never identified, and we are left with a structure, a "return," or turning back, from inviolability into defeat.

Peripeteia, as Kenner uses the word, is movement caught at the still point of a turn. In "The Return" the movement from confident advance to troubled retreat is defined by the structure at that still point, a particular structure of a particular kind of unexpected change. An Image in which the structure defines a *peripeteia*, then, is a further form of the "moving Image," and a further way in which phanopoeia catches up time and action. Without that structure the poem would be only a description of a work of art, and, like the scene Keats saw on the Grecian urn, a cold pastoral, a moment frozen out of time into eternity. Phanopoeia can of course do that as well. Curiously, the image of the snow caught in a turn of the wind is a key element of what makes this poem something different. As another *peripeteia* seen behind the turning back of the hunters, it tells us something about the hesitating, murmuring way they turn back, and something about the nature of whatever force it was that has turned them back.

A third version of the "moving Image" is seen in two poems by William Carlos Williams. The first poem, in fact, is an explicit lesson on the form of Image that characterizes Williams' poetry, as well as a lesson on introducing a sense of the kinetic into that form:

To a Solitary Disciple

Rather notice, mon cher,
that the moon is
tilted above
the point of the steeple
than that its color
is shell-pink.

Rather observe
that it is early morning
than that the sky
is smooth
as a turquoise.

Rather grasp
how the dark
converging lines
of the steeple
meet at the pinnacle—
perceive how
its little ornament
tries to stop them—

See how it fails!
See how the converging lines
of the hexagonal spire
escape upward—
receding, dividing!
—sepals
that guard and contain
the flower!

Observe
how motionless
the eaten moon
lies in the protecting lines.

It is true:
in the light colors
of morning

brown-stone and slate
shine orange and dark blue.

But observe
the oppressive weight
of the squat edifice!
Observe
the jasmine lightness
of the moon.
                    (*Collected Earlier Poems*, pp. 167-68)

In this poem William Carlos Williams gives us both a poetics of the Image and a demonstration of that poetics. Or
perhaps it would be more accurate to call it a physics of
the Image, for it is concerned less with the juxtaposed
elements in the Image than with the alignment of forces
generated by that juxtaposition. The "solitary disciple"
(this is not going to be a popular way of writing poetry)
is told first of all to practice an increasing clarity of vision:
"notice," then "observe," then "grasp." The objective, however, is not precise description of the moon, the church
steeple, or the sky, but a perception of relationships. What
is to be seen is not the color of the moon but its position
"tilted above / the point of the steeple," not the turquoise
smoothness of the sky but the time of day seen in that sky,
not the fact that we have a church steeple with a cross on
top but the forces of the lines of the steeple as they break
through the obstructing mass of the "little ornament." For
now, at least, we are no more interested in thoughts about
the soaring or obstructing characteristics of the Christian

religion than we are in the secondary qualities of color and surface in the objects we are observing. Rather, see the basic qualities of the Image:

"notice"	$\longrightarrow$	POSITION	(x,y,z)
"observe"	$\longrightarrow$	TIME	(t)
"grasp"	$\longrightarrow$	FORCE/MOTION	$(F=ma)$

Along the way the poet shows, perhaps for the disciple's benefit, that he can do the image of precise description, if he wants to, and do it very well:

> It is true:
> in the light colors
> of morning
>
> brown-stone and slate
> shine orange and dark blue.

Also, his perception of the relationship of the moon and the steeple has incidentally brought him a metaphor, an additional juxtaposition in his Image: the moon lies in the projected lines of the steeple like a flower in its sepals. He will use this—another poet searched a long time for the image of petals on a wet, black bough—but this poet finds these less interesting than the basics of position, time, and force.

Although we have time to observe the moon lying motionless in the protecting lines of the steeple, forces are still in motion and the Image does not remain at rest. We have observed the time: since the moon is still up in the early morning, it is in its waning phase, having been "eaten" night by night. At this point in the poem we might expect it to set, to fall through the protecting lines to the horizon. But it does not; they hold. Then in the last stanza the poet shows the disciple that in addition to spatial position and time another fundamental aspect of nature, gravity, is also seen in the Image, and he finishes the Image by setting it in motion. The "squat edifice" (a church, but, like the cross, that is not important here) pushes down in this stanza with "oppressive weight." There is however a contrary force in the "jasmine lightness" of the moon. The phrase is drawn in part from the flower/moon image noticed earlier, but "jasmine" is also a scent, the perfume as well as the flower, and the Image is completed as the moon begins to move away in an unexpected direction, evaporating into the sky as the morning grows brighter around it. ("Poetry," Pound once wrote, "is in some odd way concerned with the specific gravity of things, with their nature.")[14] In this poem Williams teaches his lone disciple first how to resolve appearances into structured forces and then how to let the resolution of those forces set the Image in motion.

Although they do it in different ways, Pound and Williams both introduce a sense of the kinetic into the structure of the Image. It is the structure that is essential: for both poets it is seeing the forces in the structure of the Image that leads to seeing the movements those forces define. This is the lesson of "To a Solitary Disciple," and the lesson is applied in "Spring Strains":

> In a tissue-thin monotone of blue-grey buds
> crowded erect with desire against the sky
>   tense blue-grey twigs
> slenderly anchoring them down, drawing
> them in—
>
>   two blue-grey birds chasing
> a third struggle in circles, angles,
> swift convergings to a point that bursts
> instantly!
>
>   Vibrant bowing limbs
> pull downward, sucking in the sky
> that bulges from behind, plastering itself
> against them in packed rifts, rock blue
> and dirty orange!

Early buds are straining skyward toward the "rock blue /

and dirty orange" clouds of a New Jersey spring. But there is a root-force pulling downward, anchoring the buds through the twigs, holding the birds in swift orbits about the tree, and through the bowing limbs sucking down the cloudy sky itself. The circling orbits and the downward pull through all the elements of the tree are the basis of the Image here, not the painterly blue-grey of the buds or the blues and oranges of the sky. Against the actions of this downward root-force is set a contrary force:

> But—
> (Hold hard, rigid jointed trees!)
> the blinding and red-edged sun-blur—
> creeping energy, concentrated
> counterforce—welds sky, buds, trees,
> rivets them in one puckering hold!
> Sticks through! Pulls the whole
> counter-pulling mass upward, to the right
> locks even the opaque, not yet defined
> ground in a terrific drag that is
> loosening the very tap-roots!

As we move through this section the poem becomes almost too explicit in discussing its own structure. The "creeping energy, concentrated / counterforce" grows stronger and stronger as the spring sun breaks through the clouds. The light is a visible manifestation of the force spreading over the sky and landscape and pulling against the root-force of the first section. The resolution of these forces comes in the last stanza, not in any interpretive statement about the irresistible strength of the waxing spring sun but in the movement of the Image:

> On a tissue-thin monotone of blue-grey buds
> two blue-grey birds, chasing a third,
> at full cry! Now they are
> flung outward and up—disappearing suddenly!
> (*Collected Earlier Poems*, p. 159)

87

The eye returns to the first section of the poem, but the contained forces have suddenly become exploding forces. The circling orbits of the birds are broken and they are thrown outward and upward, flung out of the poem. The movement is powerful and violent compared to the subtle, unexpected way the moon began to move out of "To a Solitary Disciple," but the principles of the "moving Image," we see, are the same in both poems.

It is interesting to notice that in general the Image of Williams appears more frankly mimetic than does Pound's. That is, in the Williams poems the Image structure is seen in nature itself, whereas Pound's poems seem to bring together in the Image elements that were not seen together in nature. But there is really no essential difference; Pound's poems see things that should be seen together, and Williams' poems see an Image in things that are together. Both poets present structures of the visual imagination—neither a description of nature nor an imaginary nature, but a seeing into nature. A work of the imagination, Williams wrote, is "not 'like' anything but transfused with the same forces which transfuse the earth—at least one small part of them" (*Spring & All*, p. 53). In "To a Solitary Disciple" and in "Spring Strains" Williams does not describe natural motion so much as he sets the Image in motion—though it would probably be more accurate to say of both poets, since it is done through the forms of phanopoeia, that they set the motion in Image.

The second aspect of incorporating time and action in the structure of the Image is less a different method from the first than a difference of emphasis. The "timeless moment" is an effect attendant on the "moving Image," and it emphasizes that time, as well as movement, is set in Image. It is the effect Coleridge had in mind when he spoke of poetic imagery "reducing multitude to unity, or succession to an instant," an effect he felt in Shakespeare's *Venus and Adonis* "when, with more than the power of the paint-

er, the poet gives us the liveliest image of succession with
the feeling of simultaneousness" (*Biog. Lit.*, II, 16, 18). It
seems to be that "precise instant," in Pound's phrase, in
which the Image transforms itself by darting inward.

We can distinguish two ways, it seems to me, in which
poetry of the Image works toward that sense of timelessness.
The first way, well described by Coleridge as reducing succession to an instant, is a kind of differential calculus in
the language of poetry through which all the meaning of a
wide arc of time is caught in the instantaneous Image. This
is the way of Shōha's haiku which catches all the movement
of the world's turning into spring within the moment of
the stork's one pace, the way of Buson's "candle" haiku
which catches another large meaning of spring within the
moment of passing on the light, and the way of Ryōta's
poem which catches the long development of a guest-host
relationship in that silent moment of the white chrysanthemum. It is also the way of Pound's sudden discovery
in "Pagani's, November 8," the way of the *peripeteia* in
"The Return," and, at a further stage of complexity, the
way of Williams in "Bird":

> Bird with outstretched
> wings poised
> inviolate unreaching
>
> yet reaching
> your image this November
> planes
>
> to a stop
> miraculously fixed in my
> arresting eyes[15]

The poem is both an Image poem and a commentary on a
poetics of the Image; it is also, we soon notice, a riddle
poem full of paradoxes and syntactical puns. The subject
of the poem is the timeless moment of the Image, or more
precisely, the action of the timeless moment of the Image,

or even more precisely, seeing the action of the timeless moment of the Image. Most of the poem is a description of how the whole process takes place. Two words, however —"this November"—provide the necessary juxtapositions which transform the poem from a simple, though precise, description of an experience into a poem of the Image. It is not much, but exactly enough. In a bad month for birds, when many of them have already left town, a bird in November—which means November trees, with a November sky behind them—stands poised, caught and balanced at a point just before motion. *This* November—not another November; yet the word remembers and acknowledges that there have been and will be other Novembers. But for the instant the bird is poised "inviolate"; not touched; unreaching. Yet reaching, for it is November. Those spaces of time, this November and other Novembers, are both excluded from and included in the still, tense instant of the Image. The speaker sees then: the bird's image "planes / to a stop"; he also sees: "this November / planes / to a stop"; and he finally sees: "your image this November / planes / to a stop"—action and time, set in complex Image, "miraculously [no, it's just the ol' power of phanopoeia] fixed."

The other way to a sense of timelessness in poetry of the Image involves a much more explicit use of time past and time future. It is the spatialization of time which I suggested was one of the significant developments of phanopoeia in the emblem books. In Quarles' *Hieroglyphics of the Life of Man* the verses emphasizing the passage of time were seen to be part of a larger pattern in which time, rather than flowing, was caught up in spatial form. The transformation of time into picture and space is seen in the Image as well. The whole idea of the Image is visual structure, which implies simultaneity and spatial pattern. If the inherent tendency of phanopoeia to reduce motion to stasis is often a danger for the language of poetry, the ways in which the Image can contain time within space, can circum scribe movement, flow, and energy, are also particular beauties of this poetic power. The literal, pictorial sense of "space" is important to this power of the Image, though finally less important than what happens in the spaces of the visual imagination. Even in the emblem books, where there is literal, pictorial space in the plates, what was most interesting and revealing to us was the transformation of visual space into the "ideas" of conceptual space.

In Quarles' *Hieroglyphics*, and again in the poems of William Carlos Williams, the forms of phanopoeia were particularly rich because they were handled both thematically and technically, with the poetics of the poem a way of expressing what the poem is about. We look next at three poems which do the same thing with the sense of time caught in space. The first two are translations of Chinese poems, through which we approach a poem by Yeats and our final example of the powers of phanopoeia in the language of poetry. In this translation of "A Brief but Happy Meeting with My Brother-in-Law" by Li Yi (d. 827), we see long periods of time caught in an essentially spatial picture:

After these ten torn wearisome years
We have met again. We were both so changed
That hearing first your surname, I thought you a stranger—
Then hearing your given name, I remembered your young
    face. . . .
All that has happened with the tides
We have told and told till the evening bell. . . .
Tomorrow you journey to Yo-chou,
Leaving autumn between us, peak after peak.[16]

The visual transformation, the conversion of time (and time of year) into spatial pattern, is primary here, though the further transformation of visual space into conceptual space is also present, and important, in the poem. The narrative of the momentary meeting and recognition first disappears into time—into the closing day, the cycles of the tides and seasons, and the long "wearisome years." In the last line, however, where autumn is seen stretched across peak after peak, time disappears in turn into the matrix of space and picture. Time swept up into the picture of distant peaks becomes a necessary part of the recognition in the poem, and of the significance of Li Yi's brief meeting with his relative.

This sort of transformation is easily done, but it is a basic method by which the power of phanopoeia catches time in space. The process is made more complex by the method of Li Shang-yin (813-858) in "The Inlaid Harp":

I wonder why my inlaid harp has fifty strings,
Each with its flower-like fret an interval of youth.
. . . The sage Chuang-tzǔ is day-dreaming, bewitched by
    butterflies,
The spring-heart of Emperor Wang is crying in a cuckoo,
Mermen weep their pearly tears down a moon-green sea,
Blue fields are breathing their jade to the sun . . .
And a moment that ought to have lasted for ever
Has come and gone before I knew.

Whatever biographical occasions Chinese commentators have seen in this poem, in English translation the subject of the poem is nothing other than the timeless moment of the Image. The poet first of all transforms time into space in the manner of Li Yi by seeing the fifty years of his life extending across the fifty-stringed "harp" (sê), each string with its movable tuning-bridge becoming "an interval of youth." Beyond this, however, are the important allusions which lie at the heart of the poem's method. The Taoist sage Chuang-tzǔ once dreamed that he was a butterfly, and then he awoke as a man again. His lines on this experience usually hover in the background when butterflies appear in Chinese and Japanese poetry:

Am I a man who dreamed of being a butterfly,
    or am I a butterfly dreaming myself to be a man?

The next allusion refers to the legendary Emperor Wang of Shu, who died of shame after a love affair with his prime minister's wife; his spirit entered a cuckoo, where it continued to cry out longingly in the spring song of the bird. There are various interpretations of the next line in the Chinese, but this translation associates it with a legend that the tears of mermen (or mermaids) become pearls. Finally, the "Blue fields" are the jade fields of Indigo Mountain, which are said to give off their colors under the sun's heat in a mist like evaporating dew.[17]

The importance of these allusions lies in what they do to time, in the way they set up intersections of the temporal with the timeless. The allusions reach back not to the linear time of history but to the timelessness of myth and fable, to archaic models which can be integrated into the present moment and lift that moment out of the linear flow of historical time into timelessness. There is a state of mind, a space in the imagination, in which "It has happened before, and it is happening again" is seen transformed into simply "It is happening"—not again, but still. In Li Shang-yin's poem each allusion recalls a metamorphosis, a transformation from one state to another, just as the speaker in the poem is momentarily transformed from one state of consciousness to another. His experience, then, is caught in timeless models of transformation. In the ordinary time of human experience the moment "that ought to have lasted for ever" is soon gone, yet, by integration with the allusions, the poetry has fixed that moment so that it *does* last forever, lifted from the present into mythic timelessness. As Charles Olson said of Melville, the Chinese poet has reached "back through time until he got history pushed back so far he turned time into space."[18] To say that the moment has been "spatialized" may not be quite accurate, at least not in the simpler visual sense of Li Yi's poem. What has happened, however, here as in the emblem books, is that a process that begins with visual space has moved finally inward to open conceptual spaces in the imagination.

The inlaid harp is a convenient emblem of this process. First seen as a spatial image of the speaker's years, it is also the agent that begins the transformation of his vision, and after the vision is broken it remains before him as a visual reminder of a certain way of seeing. The wind-harp of the Romantic poets was also an emblem for the transforming power of the imagination: it sang the random moods of nature's winds, and when the winds died the song died as well. Li Shang-yin's harp, however, is something quite different. It is not even played; instead, it is seen—an elaborately wrought Chinese instrument seen as the poem's powers of transforming a brief vision into the timeless space of art.

Yeats was interested in all this, as we see in a final complication of the roots of phanopoeia:

The Magi

Now as at all times I can see in the mind's eye,
In their stiff, painted clothes, the pale unsatisfied ones
Appear and disappear in the blue depth of the sky
With all their ancient faces like rain-beaten stones,
And all their helms of silver hovering side by side,
And all their eyes still fixed, hoping to find once more,
Being by Calvary's turbulence unsatisfied,
The uncontrollable mystery on the bestial floor.

The poem begins, as the Chinese poem does, with a sudden vision, a momentary transformation of the speaker's normal way of seeing. Also as in the Chinese poem, the timelessness of mythic models is integrated into the present moment of the sudden vision. Li Shang-yin's timeless moment which visits him and then departs is set in a perspective of legends of other transformations; each one comes unsought, and each one brings with it, it seems, a touch of melancholy. Yeats, however, who very much sought his epiphanic moments, sees his vision set not against timeless models of unsought metamorphoses but against the model of a sacred quest. The vision is seen in the blue spaces of the sky, but the transformation into timelessness, the poet knows, happens inwardly, "in the mind's eye," in spaces created in the imagination. In those spaces the moment—and the quest of the Magi—happens "Now as at all times": like the opening formula of Old Testament narratives, "In those days, at this time," it is a formula that suggests the ever-present nature of mythic acts.

For Yeats, however, eternity often had a leak in the bottom, and in "The Magi" he has been more complex than Li Shang-yin by juxtaposing the temporal with the timeless within the mythic model itself. The "mythic model," that is, is itself an Image, and it is an Image that contains time and action. In the second line of the poem the Magi appear in "stiff, painted clothes," stylized figures as if from a Byzantine icon. The stylization and the Byzantine associations, along with the "helms of silver," are Yeats's way of reaching into the timelessness of sacred art. But set against this is the image of the Magi "With all their ancient faces like rain-beaten stones." These stones come not from an eternal Byzantium of gold and silver artifice but from a real city in which time is constantly eroding the present into the past. The two images, the Byzantine figures and the rain-beaten stones, intersect in an Image which includes both trance and transience. The mythic model itself is not quite able to hold time caught in space, and thus it is a good model for the vision of a poet who was always uncertain about his ability to hold time in the artifices of the imagination. In "The Magi" the quest is ever-present but it is also ever-unsatisfied and ever-transforming. Looking back, the goal of the quest is the "bestial floor" of Christ's manger; looking ahead, it is likely to be the lair of some rough beast that has slouched into Bethlehem to be born. Both are seen at once, I think, and both Yeats and Li Shang-yin apprehend in these poems Eliot's sense that "all time is eternally present." Yeats, however, though he caught time past and time future in the blue depth of his vision, also saw in that vision the fragility and vulnerability built into such ways of seeing.

In both Yeats and Li Shang-yin time and action caught and held in the spaces of the imagination is a much fuller process than simply stopping time and reducing motion to stasis. Lessing wrote that the single moment is the domain of the painter, whereas in poetry the individual moment is lost in the effect of the continuous whole (*Laocoon*, p. 21). Here, however, is a power in poetry that tries to hold on to the individual moment. "When we name it, life exists" —in a space created in the imagination. Yeats and Li Shang-yin named their momentary experiences by integrating into them timeless models, and by thus naming them made them exist. Providing models for temporal human experience is a function that myth has always served, and the power of phanopoeia in the language of poetry gives us a technical explanation, rather than the more common metaphysical or sociological explanations, for the attraction of modern poets to myths, especially to myths of metamorphosis. Such a distinction, however, ultimately does not satisfy, for we also recognize the truth of Sister M. Bernetta Quinn's explanation of attempts on the part of poets such as Yeats, Pound, Eliot, and even Williams to catch the transience of historical moments in the net of mythic metamorphoses: metamorphosis, she writes, is "one resolution of the question of transience, since in the cyclic character of the universe, 'All things doo chaunge. But nothing sure dooth perish.' (Golding's Ovid.) Ezra Pound, particularly, has stressed this apparent immortality which the absolute confers upon beauty, drawn forth time and time again in fresh media. Such a thesis is perhaps as close as writers like Pound come to the supernatural, this insistence upon perfection waiting and longing to break through the façade of the quotidian."[19]

I have suggested two ways by which the Image works toward a sense of timelessness and a space for fuller knowing: the differential calculus of haiku, Pound's short Image poems, and Williams' "Bird," and the (may Blake forgive us) integral calculus of Yeats and Li Shang-yin. Both ways finally involve metamorphosis. Metamorphosis is a juxtaposition of two forms of the same thing; man into beast or man into god still carries, in the old myths, his human identity into the new form. We began with Moritake's Image of a falling blossom and a rising butterfly and with Pound's Image of subway riders and petals. These short poems can be seen as Images that catch metamorphosis at a crucial point. Earl Miner has written of Moritake's poem that in a sense the poet *did* see the fallen blossom return to the bough: "He has witnessed one of nature's metamorphoses; the flowers fell, and arose, so to speak, in a new incarnation. Beauty of one kind passes by changing into beauty of another form."[20] And Hugh Kenner, on the "timeless moment" which Pound labored for more than a year to catch in an Image: "The brevity of Imagist notation seized phenomena just on the point of mutating, as in the most famous example an apparition of faces turns into petals. Misrepresented as a poetic of stasis, it had been a poetic of darting change . . ." (*The Pound Era*, p. 367). It was Wallace Stevens who, in *The Necessary Angel*, was unsure whether to call this power in the poet's language metaphor or metamorphosis.

Poetry, one poet has written recently, "can make-things-present by naming them."[21] I take this in two senses. One sense has to do with the "calling" of names, and the calling of things or of powers in things from there to here or from here to there. This sort of naming is the subject of chapter six. In the other sense, naming makes things present by bringing time and action into the present tense of the Image, and that has been the subject of this chapter. It is seen in the energies of Pound's precise juxtapositions, in Williams' resolution of forces into motion, in time caught through the differential calculus of the instantaneous Image and through the integral calculus of myth and metamorphosis. Naming in this sense is first of all a seeing, but a seeing that is done with more than the eye. If we say instead, as Pound does, that it is done with "the visual imagination" we begin to recognize, or to acknowledge, that seeing is a creative and not a passive act. It is not simply recording impressions, but creating and structuring complex spaces in the imagination. The kind of seeing we are interested in is a way of knowing. In the riddle, the emblem, and the Image, the power to catch and hold time and action in the spaces of the imagination is essential to the act of naming, for time, process, and movement are essential characteristics of most things worth knowing. Phanopoeia's way of seeing them, of knowing them, and of naming them in a poem is to contain them in the active patterns of spatial and conceptual form.

Naming is of course an act of language, and phanopoeia a way of charging language with meaning. For phanopoeia, names are the consequences of things, but not the thing itself; the poet's language intervenes. The riddle, in folklore and in sophisticated poetry, is a naming, a seeing of the unknown ("aging man") in terms of the known ("autumn tree"). But it is not an equation: the unknown does not completely fit into the known, and rather than simply substituting one word for another the poet finds a naming that opens a space in which "autumn tree," "aging man," the attractions of the similarities and the tensions of the differences, are all part of a further definition of the name "man." The emblematists tried to present those spaces of the imagination with the visual spaces of their engraved plates and woodcuts, but in the end the plates became only one component of the language of the emblem method. In Quarles' *Hieroglyphics* the emblem method is a three-part juxtaposition of the visual plate, the verses, and the motto. Again a space is created in which the unknown ("life of man") is seen in terms of the known ("burning candle"), a space that contains the movements and paradoxes of both the "fit" and the "non-fit." In the Image as well a complex and dynamic structure of images, emotions, paradoxes, forces, and movements is seen and known and named. For convenience we may at times designate that space with a familiar word ("spring," "loneliness," "freedom," "friendship," "courage," "defeat," "rebirth"), but when we do so we have a name emptied of the active power of naming. Phanopoeia, then, is a power in language for accurate naming, and the poet's job is to make present to the reader's imagination all the visual precisions, the paradoxical structures, and the complex, "caught-time" spaces that an accurate naming must include. *Hoc opus, hic labor est.* Perhaps it has been that labor which has led poets to dream of finding what they now must make: a language that reveals rather than conceals the right names for things, a language that is itself charged from the roots up with the powers of phanopoeia.

V. IDEOGRAM

> Here I lay a spot of red paint down on my canvas.
> Next I choose a green which I dot near it. The red is
> immediately changed, and so is the green. In con-
> trast to the green the red has taken fire, and the
> green now glows inwardly like an emerald. The re-
> action is mutual. . . .
>
> —*Ernest Fenollosa, "The Logic of Art" (1906)*

IN JULY OF 1878 Ernest Fenollosa, a young New Englander
from Salem, sailed from America to take up a teaching
position in Japan. Born in 1853, the year Perry had pried
open Japanese ports for American trade, Fenollosa had
studied philosophy at Harvard (Class of '74), had remained
there for two years following his graduation as a resident
fellow in philosophy, had then drifted into divinity school
for a while, and had just spent the previous year studying
painting and drawing. Japan in 1878 was modernizing itself
along Western lines, and Fenollosa was offered the first
chair of philosophy at the new Tokyo University. He did
teach Western philosophy when he arrived in Japan, but he
also discovered there an artistic tradition so rich and, he
felt, so superior to the Western art of the nineteenth century that he turned his abilities to the study and preserva-
tion of traditional Japanese art. During later extended stays
in Japan Fenollosa became interested in translating Japanese and Chinese literature, and in the midst of many other
projects he began to make notes on the Japanese Nō plays
and on Chinese poetry and poetics. He died suddenly on a
visit to London in 1908, however, and that work was never
finished.[1]

From the many manuscripts and notes that Fenollosa left, his widow, Mary Fenollosa, completed his major work, the two-volume *Epochs of Chinese and Japanese Art,* which was published in London in 1912. A year later she turned over to Ezra Pound her husband's manuscripts on Oriental poetry and drama. Working from these manuscripts, Pound turned the translations of Chinese poetry into *Cathay* (1915), and the translations of Japanese Nō drama into '*Noh*'—*or, Accomplishment* (1916). After some difficulty in finding a publisher, he placed Fenollosa's speculations on poetics in *The Little Review* in 1919, and a year later he included them in his book *Instigations of Ezra Pound.* They appeared under the title Fenollosa had given them as a set of lecture notes, *The Chinese Written Character as a Medium for Poetry.*

For Pound, Fenollosa's essay on the Chinese written character was a revelation; it seemed to confirm and to justify his theories of the poetic Image, and it also led him to the "ideogrammic method" of *The Cantos.* For us, Fenollosa's essay is the culmination and conclusion of our discussion of phanopoeia in the language of lyric poetry. Fenollosa saw preserved in the Chinese character all the powers of phanopoeia that we have been seeking out. The character has a visual basis. It works with juxtapositions that unite seeing and knowing at the rock-bottom level of the word. It encompasses time and action, forces and movements, within an essentially spatial form. It is a naming.

The Chinese Written Character as a Medium for Poetry is one of the high points of modern poetics, though this opinion is far from unanimous. When the aim of the essay is misunderstood it can appear to be a fanciful and incompetent work on Chinese linguistics. When the aim of the essay is understood it can still generate suspicion or worse in literary critics. Since the dust of controversy is still settling, I propose that we step carefully up to this small book, first by examining briefly what the ideogram is and how it works in the Chinese written language. Then we will look at what it meant to Pound, for it has been his views that have most strongly influenced the composition of modern poems and exercised the discussions of modern poetics. Pound, however, is not our main concern, and we will finally take up Fenollosa's essay itself. We begin, then, with the ideogram in Chinese, and some general observations which, though they need many qualifications and exceptions, seem to be more or less true. The first qualification is that they are more true of the literary language of classical Chinese poetry than of the colloquial Chinese languages spoken today.[2]

A basic fact of the Chinese written character, and one that immediately engages our ideas of phanopoeia, is that unlike the fundamentally phonetic alphabets of Western languages the character represents a meaning rather than a sound. Classical Chinese is a dead language, the sounds of which can be reconstructed only through elaborate linguistic techniques, yet Chinese poetry from that period can still be read, even without any idea of its sound. It did sound, of course, and it possessed a fully developed system of versification built on the music of tone, syllable-count, and rhyme. But while the sounds of spoken Chinese changed with the passing centuries, and much of the original music of the poetry was lost, the meaning associated with a written character remained relatively constant. This is an advantage of character-writing that remains in Chinese up to the present day: although a man from Peking would have considerable difficulty in speaking to a man from Canton, they could "read" each other perfectly. Their spoken words for the concept of loyalty, for example, might be entirely different, but they would both represent it in writing with the same character. Every Chinese character, in theory at least, presents a meaning visually rather than phonetically, and, still speaking generally, one character represents one word. Speaking more strictly, a character corresponds to a syllable, and compounds—two-syllable words represented by two characters—do occur. But the language of the classical poetry is generally monosyllabic, with a five-character line representing a line of five monosyllabic words.

Thus it is the visual form of the Chinese character that is important, rather than the sound of the word represented by the character. Visual form, however, is not the same thing as "picture," for Chinese characters are not pictograms resembling the objects and concepts they represent. While this may be true historically of the most basic words in the written language, which began as a type of hieroglyphic picture-writing, it is not, Bernhard Karlgren observed, a technique that could have taken the language very far (*The Chinese Language*, p. 10). This became a particularly troublesome point between Sinologists and Pound, who, because he was mainly interested in the ideogram, could give the impression that he thought every character was an ideogram and every ideogram was made up of a combination of pictorial elements. Traditional Chinese etymology is more precise, giving six principles, the "Six Scripts," which underlie the structure of the characters. Four of the principles have to do with the formation of characters, and it is to these we look to understand how a character presents a meaning.

The first principle of character formation was "Imitating the Form," the creation of *simple pictograms* which at first were attempts to picture a meaning. Thus one of the modern characters for "man" 人 is a stylization of an early picture of a man walking on his two legs, and it is still possible to see in the modern character for "tree" 木 a tree trunk with its spreading branches. The second principle, "Pointing at the Thing," created *simple ideograms* to represent abstract concepts. A line across the top of the "tree" character gave the character for "tree-top" 末, which then took on the meanings of "tip" or "end," applied to anything. Putting the line at the bottom of the "tree" character, pointing to the root of the tree, produced the character for "basis," "origin," or "source" 本. The third principle, "Understanding the Meaning," combined two or more simple characters into a new character, a *composite ideogram*, to make a new meaning. Placing the character for "pig" 豕 under the character for "roof" 宀 produced the character for "house," "home," "family" 家 . It was this method of character formation that most excited Pound, for its juxtaposition of two concrete images to create a new meaning seemed to him to be the essence of the Image.

The composite ideogram was still too limited for a complete written language, however, and a majority of the characters in Chinese are derived from a fourth principle, "Harmonizing the Sound," or the creation of a *composite phonogram*. This method was a step toward phonetic representation of the language, for it took a character which had some relationship with the meaning of the new word and combined it with the character for a word which at that time sounded the same as the new word. The component related to the meaning is usually called the *signific*, or *radical*, and the component related to the sound is called the *phonetic*. Thus the character for "to beat" 扣 combined the radical for "hand" 扌 with the phonetic taken from the character for "mouth" 口 , both "to beat" and "mouth" being pronounced *$k'u$ at the time of the formation of the character. The resulting compound showed that the new word involved something done with the hand, while it sounded like *$k'u$, the word for "mouth." This method, Karlgren wrote, was well suited to the Chinese language, which, being so largely monosyllabic, contained many homophones:

> By combining already existing graphs in pairs, one of which functioned as phonetic and the other as signific, new signs could be devised practically without limit. There was a framework, a stock of simple graphs, which, combined in pairs according to this principle, could easily and quickly denote any other word which in itself would be difficult to depict. In rapid sequence hundreds and thousands of such half-

ideographic, half-phonetic compounds were created,
and in fact nine tenths of all Chinese characters are
constructed according to this principle.   (p. 13)

Since it is difficult to spend a day, much less years, in con-
tact with Chinese characters without realizing that a large
number of the characters contain a phonetic element, it is
simply not reasonable to suppose that either Pound or
Fenollosa was unaware of the composite phonogram. Yet
the presence of what was originally a phonetic sign in
many characters clearly means that those characters cannot
be traced back to a juxtaposition of two images; they go
back to the combining of an image and a sound.[3] Before
we take up Pound's and Fenollosa's ways of seeing the Chinese character, however, we must look briefly at how the
characters are joined to present the larger meanings of a
phrase, a sentence, or a line of poetry.

When Pound, following Fenollosa's notes, turned to Chinese poetry he found a poetic language which seemed to
embody his principles of juxtaposition far more fundamentally than the English, Provençal, Latin, Greek, or other
Western languages with which he had been working. James
Liu shows that a line from a poem by Wei Chuang (836?-
910), which would have to be expressed in English as "Like
frost or frozen snow her white wrists shine," stands in the
Chinese as a five-character line which, translated literally,
reads simply "Bright wrist frozen frost snow" (*The Art of
Chinese Poetry*, p. 31). The basically monosyllabic nature
of literary Chinese excludes inflections that would designate
the tense of verbs or the number and case of nouns. Also,
connective verbs and personal pronouns are often dropped.
As a result, the grammar of a line is implicitly contained in
word-order patterns or in function words, not explicitly
mapped with declensions and conjunctions. Hsieh Wen
Tung is clearer about all this:

the absence of tenses, of personal pronouns and con-
nectives, is relative, and such relative absence does not

105

imply a lack of grammar. Chinese is an uninflected language and its grammar contextual rather than explicit. The word being an integral character rather than an alphabetical group, it cannot carry suffixes or prefixes to indicate its mutations in function. In English *red* as an adjective and as a noun remains the same, but as a verb it is *to redden*; as gerund and present participle *reddening*, as past participle *reddened*; in Chinese *hung* would have to stand for them all. Its function would be determined by its position in the sentence, its significance defined by the context. Similarly, tenses would have to be indicated by particles before the verb or at the end of the sentence; or, as more generally, and in poetry especially, by the use of adverbs of time.[4]

Chinese critics are not above giving us some speculations of their own about the nature of their written language as a medium for poetry. The lack of precise indications of verb tense, Hsieh Wen Tung suggests, poses no obstacle to lyric poetry, for exact time relationships are not so important in lyric as they might be in narrative or dramatic poetry: "For the purposes of exposition—or of non-narrative and non-dramatic poetry—distinctions between the past, present and future kept in any way will suffice. Where they are not needed the tense-inflections are better absent, for their absence helps to the view of things *sub specie aeternitatis*" (p. 414). James Liu speculates that the ambiguity of number in nouns is also an asset that helps poetry to concentrate on the universal, as in the line: "The moonrise surprises the mountain bird (or birds)." In poetry, one bird will do as well as several. The classical poetry also avoided the use of personal pronouns, and Liu writes that leaving out the "I" of the speaker

allows the poet not to intrude his own personality upon the scene, for the missing subject can be readily identified with anyone, whether the reader or some imaginary person. Consequently, Chinese poetry often has an impersonal and universal quality, compared with which much Western poetry appears egocentric and earthbound. Where Wordsworth wrote "*I* wander*ed* lonely as *a* cloud," a Chinese poet would probably have written simply "Wander as cloud." The former records a personal experience bound in space and time; the latter presents a state of being with universal applications.

(pp. 40-41)

We can be grateful for the insights these comments give us into the workings of language in Chinese poetry without subscribing to the general views of poetry implicit in them. They help us to see what the nature of a written line of Chinese poetry is, whether or not that line is, or should be, timeless, impersonal, or universal.

James Liu's study of Chinese poetry is helpful once more by giving us two translations of a lyric by Ma Chih-yuan (ca. 1270-1330), a literal translation and a verse translation. The original is a five-line poem with three six-character lines, a four-character line, and a final six-character line. With the addition of some inflections, a literal character-by-character crib of the poem runs like this:

> Withered vines old trees twilight crows
> Little bridge flowing water people's house
> Ancient road west wind lean horse
> Evening sun west set
> Broken-bowel man at heaven end

The verse translation is:

> Withered vines, aged trees, twilight crows.
> Beneath the little bridge by the cottage the river flows.
> On the ancient road and lean horse the west wind blows.
> The evening sun westward goes,
> As a broken-hearted man stands at heaven's close.

(pp. 32-33)

To be fair about it, the verse translation was committed to preserving the rhyme scheme of the original. A reader looking for the roots of lyric would object not to this but to the way the verse translation binds the energies of the images into the syntax of prose interpretation, a limitation which the images heartily resist. The literal translation, in contrast, presents terse, concrete juxtapositions. In it are patterns of overlapping forms; tensions, movements, and time caught in a structure; and a complex naming of sorrow.

Pound, then, saw Chinese poetry coming over into English as a juxtaposition of visually presented words standing without much of the logical predication that works as connective tissue in English poetry. He was less interested in universality than in a poetic language that could present a "direct treatment of the thing"—

| cock | crow | thatch | inn | moon |
| man | trace | wood | bridge | frost |

—or "objects in their purest form uncontaminated by intellect or subjectivity," as Wai-lim Yip, who translates these lines, puts it (*Ezra Pound's* Cathay, p. 25). The lines involve an early-morning journey, the low moon still visible in the sky, footprints in the frost covering a wooden bridge —and they come into English as a juxtaposition of ten nouns precisely seen and set together. Phrases, as well as individual words, appear to be set one against the other in what Yip calls "syntactically uncommitted resemblance":

floating cloud (s)   wanderer ('s) thought (mood)
setting sun   old friend ('s) feeling   (p. 21)

The floating clouds are set beside the thoughts in a wanderer's mind, the setting sun beside feelings toward an old friend. Pound kept as close as he could to these roots and translated Li Po's lines:

Mind like a floating wide cloud,
Sunset like the parting of old acquaintances.

(Personae, p. 137)

(The "like" was a concession which, ever since "In a Station of the Metro," was optional.) There is no doubt that Pound's view of these things was rather different from that of Chinese readers accustomed to the patterns of their language. He saw a language that was alive with Images, and if Chinese poets had "attained the known maximum of *phanopoeia*" (and he was sure they had), this was "due perhaps to the nature of their written ideograph" (*Literary Essays*, p. 27).

We have lightly scanned the characteristics of the Chinese written language which stand behind the critical vocabularies of Pound and Fenollosa because it is sometimes difficult to distinguish in their writings between those things offered as facts of the Chinese language and those offered only as analogies of their theories of poetry. This is a particular problem in reading Pound, whose enthusiasm for an idea led him at times to certain extravagant claims. His emphasis on the pictorial element of Chinese characters is one example:

The Egyptians finally used abbreviated pictures to represent sounds, but the Chinese still use abbreviated pictures AS pictures, that is to say, Chinese ideogram does not try to be the picture of a sound, or to be a written sign recalling a sound, but it is still the picture of a thing; of a thing in a given position or relation, or of a combination of things. It *means* the thing or the action or situation, or quality germane to the several things that it pictures.

Gaudier Brzeska, who was accustomed to looking at the real shape of things, could read a certain amount of

Chinese writing without ANY STUDY. He said, "Of course, you can *see* it's a horse" (or a wing or whatever).   (*ABC of Reading*, p. 7)

It is possible that Gaudier-Brzeska could do this—he was looking, Hugh Kenner tells us, at the unsquared characters in Morrison's Dictionary (*The Pound Era*, pp. 250-51)— but because of the phonetic element in most Chinese characters it is only barely possible, and then only with a very small percentage of characters. But the basis of Pound's statement holds: a Chinese character represents a meaning rather than a sound. The rest of the statement seems to be true only of Pound's ideogram.

If Pound first saw his ideas of the Image emerging through the juxtapositions in Japanese haiku, his encounter with Chinese allowed him to take this technique in two different directions. His concept of the ideogram took it down to the level of the word itself, and his "ideogrammic method" expanded the technique to where it could structure an entire work. The first direction, as his statement above suggests, led him to treat certain individual Chinese characters as juxtapositions of discrete elements which create a new meaning through the relationships of the elements. Thus in his appendix to Fenollosa's essay on the Chinese written character Pound suggested that the character for "truth," or "sincerity" 信 , creates its meaning through the juxtaposition of the abbreviated character for "man" 亻 and the character for "word" 言 , while the "word" radical is itself created from the radical for "mouth" 口 with something (two words and a flame, guessed Fenollosa) emerging.[5] He saw the concept of sincerity, that is, expressed in Chinese writing by the visual presentation of a man standing by his word.

This way of reading a Chinese character has become known as the "split-character heresy." If it were applied to all characters it would of course go seriously wrong by treating every character as a composite ideogram and neg-